Emily Dickinson

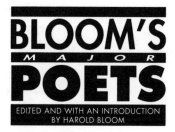

BLOOM'S
MAJOR
POETS

EDITED AND WITH AN INTRODUCTION
BY HAROLD BLOOM

Emily
Dickinson

BLOOM'S
M A J O R
POETS

EDITED AND WITH AN INTRODUCTION
BY HAROLD BLOOM

© 1999 by Chelsea House Publishers, a division of Main Line Book Co.

Introduction © 1999 by Harold Bloom

Printed and bound in the United States of America.

3 5 7 9 8 6 4 2

Library of Congress Cataloging-in-Publication Data

Emily Dickinson / edited and with an introduction by Harold Bloom.
p.   cm.— (Bloom's major poets)
Includes bibliographical references and index.
ISBN 0-7910-5106-4
1. Dickinson, Emily, 1830-1896—Examinations—Study guides.
2. Women and literature—United States—Outlines, syllabi, etc.
I. Bloom, Harold.   II. Series.
PS1541.Z5E38   1999
811'.4—dc21
98-41763
CIP

Chelsea House Publishers
1974 Sproul Road, Suite 400
Broomall, PA 19008-0914

Contributing Editor: Erica DaCosta

Contents

User's Guide

This volume is designed to present biographical, critical, and bibliographical information on the author's best-known or most important poems. Following Harold Bloom's editor's note and introduction are a detailed biography of the author, discussing major life events and important literary accomplishments. A thematic and structural analysis of each poem follows, tracing significant themes, patterns, and motifs in the work.

A selection of critical extracts, derived from previously published material from leading critics, analyzes aspects of each poem. The extracts consist of statements from the author, if available, early reviews of the work, and later evaluations up to the present. A bibliography of the author's writings (including a complete list of all books written, cowritten, edited, and translated), a list of additional books and articles on the author and the work, and an index of themes and ideas in the author's writings conclude the volume.

∼

Harold Bloom is Sterling Professor of the Humanities at Yale University and Henry W. and Albert A. Berg Professor of English at the New York University Graduate School. He is the author of over 20 books and the editor of more than 30 anthologies of literary criticism.

Professor Bloom's works include *Shelley's Mythmaking* (1959), *The Visionary Company* (1961), *Blake's Apocalypse* (1963), *Yeats* (1970), *A Map of Misreading* (1975), *Kabbalah and Criticism* (1975), and *Agon: Toward a Theory of Revisionism* (1982). *The Anxiety of Influence* (1973) sets forth Professor Bloom's provocative theory of the literary relationships between the great writers and their predecessors. His most recent books include *The American Religion* (1992), *The Western Canon* (1994), *Omens of Millennium: The Gnosis of Angels, Dreams, and Resurrection* (1996), and *Shakespeare: The Invention of the Human,* 1998.

Professor Bloom earned his Ph.D. from Yale University in 1955 and has served on the Yale faculty since then. He is a 1985 MacArthur Foundation Award recipient and served as the Charles Eliot Norton Professor of Poetry at Harvard University in 1987–88. He is currently the editor of other Chelsea House series in literary criticism, including BLOOM'S NOTES, BLOOM'S MAJOR SHORT STORY WRITERS, MAJOR LITERARY CHARACTERS, MODERN CRITICAL VIEWS, MODERN CRITICAL INTERPRETATIONS, and WOMEN WRITERS OF ENGLISH AND THEIR WORKS.

Editor's Note

My Introduction briefly comments upon the three poems of Emily Dickinson that are considered in this volume: "There's a certain Slant of light" (Poem 238), "Because I could not stop for Death" (Poem 712), and "Tell all the Truth but tell it slant" (Poem 1129).

As there are two dozen critical views excerpted here, I will mention only a few of what I take to be the high points. Formalist criticism is represented by Allen Tate, Yvor Winters, and R. P. Blackmur, while three notable poets—Richard Wilbur, Louise Bogan, and Anthony Hecht—give us the perspectives of praxis.

Dickinson's founding critics—George F. Whicher, Austin Warren, and Charles Anderson—are here. Feminist criticism is represented by Joanne Feit Diehl, Suzanne Juhasz, and Christanne Miller.

I find particularly useful some of the scholarly critics who contextualize Dickinson in her literary culture: David Porter, Shira Wolosky, Cynthia Griffin Wolff, Albert Gelpi, and Jerome McGann.

Introduction

HAROLD BLOOM

Emily Dickinson rivals Walt Whitman, Wallace Stevens, Robert Frost, T. S. Eliot, and Hart Crane; these six are the major poets thus far engendered by the United States. Like the other five, Dickinson had an antithetical relation to a central American precursor: Ralph Waldo Emerson. Emerson, neither transcendental optimist nor fatalistic pessimist, ultimately took his stand upon experience, thus fostering pragmatism. Dickinson too was a pragmatist before that American philosophy was formulated. No poet teaches more compellingly that the only differences that matter are those that make a difference. Dickinson differed from Emersonianism and differed from Calvinist Christianity. Yet she went to school with Emerson and with the poets he celebrated: Shakespeare, Milton, and Wordsworth, to whom she added Keats. Her spiritual attachments, like Emerson's, were to what she called "this loved Philology," that is, to poetry itself. The self, which is part or particle of God, is exalted by Emerson. Dickinson also had no positive use for a God external to the self. Self-reliance, both cognitive and spiritual, is as much her mode as it was Emerson's, though unlike Emerson she chose as her prime poetic subject the high cost of confirmation.

Dickinson is a very difficult poet; even her best critics tend to underestimate just how subtle and complex a body of work ensued from her immense cognitive originality. She thought through not less than everything for herself. Only Shakespeare, Milton, Blake, and Emerson can be judged to have made all things new as Dickinson did. Walt Whitman, the other major American poet of the 19th century, manifests an originality of vision comparable to Dickinson's, though his cognitive powers are not his primary endowment. Whitman perpetually surprises us by nuance, as Wallace Stevens was to do a century later. Dickinson mounts Emerson's "stairway of surprise," but with an intellectual difference:

> Surprise is like a thrilling—pungent—
> Upon a tasteless meat
> Alone—too acrid—but combined
> An edible delight.

Comic poet as she frequently is, Dickinson is unique in terming surprise a kind of acrid herb, not to be taken by itself. Her target rather genially is Emerson, from whom she had learned: "Tell all the truth but tell it slant." The Truth's superb surprise, as blinding as it is too acrid, requires mediation, a certain slant of light. Oxymoron, the rhetoric of seeming contradiction, was inherited by Dickinson from Keats, and Poem 258, with its "Heavenly Hurt" and "imperial affliction," weaves Keats's kind of sensuous apprehension into the subtle reception of a New England light that signifies mortality. The "internal difference,/Where the Meanings, are" is wholly Dickinson's own realm. Clearly this is a difference that makes a considerable difference from Emerson, and from all other forerunners. Despair is a purely Dickinsonian seal, and ambiguously can neither be instructed nor expounded by others.

Poem 258 is packed with enigmas. What takes place between the arrival and the departure of the slant of light? The listening landscape and the breathless shadows inaugurate the coming of the slant, and its going is a similitude for the distance we see on the faces of our dead. Death and the dead are Dickinson's obsessive subjects. Poem 712, "Because I could not stop for Death," is the most playful of her masterpieces in this area. Here Death comes courting, in a manner suitable for Miss Dickinson of Amherst, with Immortality serving as chaperone or duenna during the courting drive.

From the third stanza on, the journey has no precedents, and parts from ordinary categories of space and time. Erotic despair is the authentic burden of "Because I could not stop for Death," and Death is a surrogate for a lover either renounced or lost to circumstances. The tone of this lyric is extraordinarily subtle, even for Dickinson. There is no panic or alarm in her apparent abduction by a demon lover. Death's civility remains impeccable; he is the finest gentleman in Amherst. Indeed, he receives no individual mention after the second stanza. The courtship remains enthralling; centuries feel shorter than a particular day. But how should the speaker's affect be described, even as she experiences being carried off? Dickinson's tonalities are never more uncanny. The reader, teased into imagination and into thought, is given the pleasure and the perplexity of unriddling this great lyric of loss. ❀

Biography of Emily Dickinson

(1830–1886)

Emily Dickinson was born in Amherst, Massachusetts, on December 10, 1830. This fact is only one of the mere handful of certainties about the life of this reclusive poet, covered, as it was, in a "poetic veil." We know that, except for a few months of travel, she remained in Amherst until her death. And we know that Dickinson began, in her twenties, a gradual retreat into the confines of the Homestead, the house in which she was born, until for the last fifteen years of her life she did not leave its grounds and saw no one but her brother and sister.

Before Emily, there was already a strong Dickinson presence in New England. Her family, although not particularly religious, was of original Puritan stock; Emily herself never accepted Christ or the doctrine of innate sin—a fact her friends and family were aware of but accepted along with all her eccentricities. Her predecessors were Protestant "men of deeds" who worked themselves to death. Her grandfather was the driving force behind the establishment of Amherst College; he was ruined both physically and financially by his endeavors. Her father, Edward, worked tirelessly as an attorney, legislator, treasurer of Amherst College, and community leader, until he died, suddenly, in 1874.

In her youth, Emily Dickinson's home was the center of much community and academic activity. Her father customarily entertained the writers and politicians who visited Amherst College, affording Emily audience to some of the finest minds in nineteenth-century America; Ralph Waldo Emerson figured prominently among Dickinson's guests.

After studying for seven years at Amherst Academy, at the age of seventeen she went on to Mount Holyoke Female Seminary (now Mount Holyoke College), in South Hadley, Massachusetts. Whether because of homesickness, ill health, or her defiance toward the church—or because of all three—Emily returned home without ever finishing her studies.

Emily was close to her brother, Austin. When he married Susan Gilbert, a childhood friend of the Dickinsons (and particularly of Emily), his new family, living in the house next door to hers, became the center of Emily's existence. The surviving correspondence between Emily and Susan shows what some critics speculate was a homoerotic attachment to her sister-in-law. Whether sexually fulfilled or not, Emily's emotional attachment was profound. When Austin's marriage crumbled, Emily suffered cruelly. Susan's manipulative behavior poisoned more than her husband and children: it brought down the entire Dickinson establishment. The pain that her spite, her social-climbing, and her alcoholic rages caused was enormous. Lavinia, her sister, who lived to 1899, insisted that Susan hastened the deaths first of Emily and then of Austin.

Emily's mother died in 1882, after a long illness. Emily and Lavinia, who also never married, lived together in the Homestead until their deaths. Lavinia was Emily's primary means of access to the outside world.

As her withdrawal intensified, Emily's principal method of communication was through her letters, which many consider as important to her canon as her poetry. Some letters may be read as poetry in themselves; this raises the potential existence of additional Dickinson poems culled from her correspondence.

Mabel Loomis Todd, the charming and lettered wife of professor David Peck Todd, arrived in Amherst in 1881 and soon befriended the Dickinsons before she realized she was entering "a family quarrel of endless involutions." This feud became known as "The War between the Houses." Mabel Todd became Austin's mistress, confidante, and sole source of happiness until he died, in 1895. She also became instrumental in the publication of Emily's poetry after her death. She never met Emily face to face; when she visited Lavinia at the Homestead, Emily sat and listened to their conversation behind a half-open door.

In her lifetime, Emily published only seven poems. Her talent was unknown. The nearest she came to a measure of recognition was through her friendship with the literary critic Thomas Wentworth Higginson, who began his correspondence with her in 1862 and continued throughout her life. Higginson saw her intellect and her ability, but he could never completely understand the importance of her poetry. He warmly received the poems she sent him, but he discouraged her from publishing them.

Emily Dickinson died on May 15, 1886, after an illness. With help from Lavinia, Mabel Todd launched the poems into publication. Their first edition (and most thereafter) was altered with unwarranted aggressiveness; the poems, for the most part, were deliberately rewritten. It was not until 1955 that Thomas H. Johnson, the Dickinson scholar, compiled, cataloged, and edited all of her poems, creating the standard edition of Dickinson's poetry. Controversy still surrounds the several drafts of some poems, where Dickinson has left no indication of the final version.

Despite Higginson's reluctance during Dickinson's lifetime, after she died he eventually arrived at the worth of her poems and joined with Mabel Todd in her efforts to find a publisher for them. "I have the greatest desire to see you," Higginson wrote to Dickinson, "always feeling that perhaps if I could once take you by the hand I might be something to you; but till then you only enshroud yourself in a fiery mist and I cannot reach you but only rejoice in the rare sparkles of light." ❀

Thematic Analysis of
"There's a certain Slant of light" (#258)

If not the most distinguishing, despair is certainly the central theme in Emily Dickinson's poetry. Despair is what most clearly sets her apart from the Emersonian Transcendentalists, to whom she owes so much. She preoccupies herself not with the cause of psychic pain but with its spiritual aftermath; the source does not interest her, only its qualities and characteristics. In "There's a certain Slant of light," which has been classified as a nature poem, the "Slant of light" is not a description of nature; it is despair made manifest in nature. Her recurring nature images would lead a Transcendentalist to presume that this winter light was the cause of her transport, as nature implies the presence of God. It is not light that transports her, however, but pain, for which light is its metaphor in nature. A diffuse and insubstantial matter, light can be experienced only obliquely; such is the nature of despair.

Light becomes sound—the "cathedral tunes" that unequivocally "oppress." Despair remains incorporeal, as a piece of music. This unreachable despair will not change and instead changes us permanently, "the seal despair." To be sealed into despair is to ruin any chance for redemption.

A funereal atmosphere is established with the use of winter, the indirect light, and the heavy cathedral music. Dickinson shows the "internal difference" that left no scar and then returns to the winter afternoon. The sun descends and the "landscape listens" to its own demise. The fading light, which gives the landscape its existence, will extinguish all. The shadows created by the slanted light all "hold their breath" just before they extend out toward infinity, and the landscape disappears completely.

As her work often does, this poem finds references to other Dickinson poems. The figure of the setting sun, as well as shadows, reappear in #764:

> Presentiment—is that long Shadow—on the Lawn—
> Indicative that Suns go down—
>
> The Notice to the startled Grass
> That Darkness—is about to pass—

The paradoxes of painful ecstasy and ecstatic despair, named here as "heavenly hurt," are Dickinsonian trademarks and recur frequently. These contradictions allow her to speak about what otherwise would be unavoidably sentimental—pure ecstasy or undiluted despair.

There is much speculation about Emily Dickinson's specific experience of hopeless love—whether its object was Charles Wadsworth, Lord Otis, or her brother's wife, Susan Gilbert. There can be little doubt that, despite her efforts to avoid them, she experienced periods of extreme emotional intensity. In only one surviving letter is there a reference to any such experience; it is a brief mention, albeit provocative: in 1862 she wrote to Thomas Wentworth Higginson, "I had a terror—since September—I could tell none—and so I sing, as the Boy does to the Burying Ground—because I am afraid" (Emily Dickinson, *Selected Letters*, ed. Thomas H. Johnson [Cambridge: The Belknap Press of Harvard University, 1986] p. 172). It is unlikely this "terror" will ever be named; it is clear, however, that she experienced a crisis of some kind that became central to her existence as she obsessed over the details and variations of its resultant pain. "That white Sustenance—/ Despair" (#640) fed her senses.

Leaping from a "heavenly hurt" to this irredeemable despair, she articulates, in another poem (#341), the pain that leads to numbness, or spiritual death.

> After great pain, a formal feeling comes—
> The Nerves sit ceremonious, like Tombs—
> The stiff Heart questions was it He, that bore,
> And Yesterday, or Centuries before?

Pain circumvents space and time repeatedly in Dickinson's poetry. Its aftermath creates dismemberment; the nerves, the heart, and the feet are separate entities. The poem continues:

> The Feet, mechanical, go round—
> Of Ground, or Air, or Ought—
> A Wooden way
> Regardless grown,
> A Quartz contentment, like a stone—

The empty formality and the meaningless, circular movement of feet connote a sort of trance. Contentment arrives, but it is stony and cold, a sterile serenity. The "formal feeling" that comes after great pain is numbness, not sensation. The poem concludes:

This is the Hour of Lead—
Remembered, if outlived,
As Freezing persons, recollect the Snow—
First—Chill—then Stupor—then the letting go—

Dickinson's sense of loss and her sense of God coexist, however contentiously. For her, despair is the punishment for an unknown crime.

Of God we ask one favor,
That we may be forgiven—
For what, he is presumed to know—
The Crime, from us, is hidden—
Immured the whole of Life
Within a magic Prison
We reprimand the Happiness
That too competes with Heaven. (#1601)

Bitterness arises here from her feelings of estrangement from God. She asks for forgiveness but does not proclaim her guilt, for even God is ignorant of the crime. Punishment is imprisonment, but in that punishment is a bliss with which even heaven must compete. She flings happiness in the face of God.

Despite its particularly unromantic tone, "There's a certain Slant of light" reveals Dickinson's romantic sensitivity to nature. She wrote to Higginson that the "sudden light of the orchards" was one of the things that inspired her to write poetry, and she came to consider herself a connoisseur of light. She also wrote to him that the change of seasons "hurt almost like music—shifting when it ease us most." Nature in this poem becomes a vehicle for a particular kind of despair. The slant of light represents pain, the direct cause of the "heavenly hurt" that is Dickinson's spiritual emblem. Her dark, interior world kept her from the ranks of the Transcendentalists, and her Puritan sensibility restrained any tendencies toward Romanticism. Thus, attempts to align Dickinson with any specific school of thought are difficult; Dickinson never claimed to be transcendentalist, existentialist, or even overtly religious. She was without politics or philosophy. ❀

Critical Views on
"There's a certain Slant of light" (#258)

CONRAD AIKEN ON EMILY DICKINSON

[Conrad Aiken is the author of *Collected Poems, Collected Short Stories,* and *A Reviewer's ABC: Collected Criticism.*]

One can say with justice that she came to full "consciousness" at the very moment when American literature came to flower. That she knew this, there cannot be any question; nor that she was stimulated and influenced by it. One must assume that she found in her immediate environment no one of her own stature, with whom she could admit or discuss such things; that she lacked the energy or effrontery to voyage out into the unknown in search of such companionship; and that lacking this courage, and wanting this help, she became easily a prey to the then current Emersonian doctrine of mystical individualism. In this connection it is permissible to suggest that her extreme self-seclusion and secrecy was both a protest and a display—a kind of vanity masquerading as modesty. She became increasingly precious, of her person as of her thought. Vanity is in her letters—at the last an unhealthy vanity. She believes that anything she says, however brief, will be of importance; however cryptic, will be deciphered. She enjoys being something of a mystery, and she sometimes deliberately and awkwardly exaggerates it. Even in notes of condolence—for which she had a morbid passion—she is vain enough to indulge in sententiousness: as when she wrote, to a friend whose father had died on her wedding-day, "Few daughters have the immortality of a father for a bridal gift."

When we come to Emily Dickinson's poetry, we find the Emersonian individualism clear enough, but perfectly Miss Dickinson's. Henry James observed of Emerson:

> The doctrine of the supremacy of the individual to himself, of his originality and, as regards his own character, *unique* quality, must have had a great charm for people living in a society in which introspection, thanks to the want of other entertainment, played almost the part of a social resource.... There was ... much relish for the utterances of a writer who would help one to take a picturesque view of one's internal possibilities, and to find in the landscape of the soul all sorts of fine sunrise and moonlight effects.

This sums up admirably the social "case" of Miss Dickinson—it gives us a shrewd picture of the causes of her singular introversion, and it suggests that we are perhaps justified in considering her the most perfect flower of New England Transcendentalism. In her mode of life she carried the doctrine of self-sufficient individualism farther than Thoreau carried it, or the naïve zealots of Brook Farm. In her poetry she carried it, with its complement of passionate moral mysticism, farther than Emerson: which is to say that as a poet she had more genius than he. Like Emerson, whose essays must greatly have influenced her, and whose poetry, especially his gnomic poems, only a little less, she was from the outset, and remained all her life, a singular mixture of Puritan and free thinker. The problems of good and evil, of life and death, obsessed her; the nature and destiny of the human soul; and Emerson's theory of compensation. Toward God, as one of her earliest critics is reported to have said, "she exhibited an Emersonian self-possession." Indeed, she did not, and could not, accept the Puritan God at all. She was frankly irreverent, on occasion, a fact which seems to have made her editors a little uneasy—one hopes that it has not resulted in the suppression of any of her work. What she was irreverent to, of course, was the Puritan conception of God, the Puritan attitude toward Him. In "Drowning" she observes:

> The Maker's cordial visage,
>   However good to see,
> Is shunned, we must admit it,
>   Like an adversity.

—Aiken, Conrad. "Emily Dickinson." In *A Reviewer's ABC*. New York: Meridian Books, 1935.

AUSTIN WARREN ON EMILY DICKINSON

Austin Warren, professor of English at the University of Michigan, is the author of *Rage and Order* and, with René Welleck, *Theory of Literature*.

I heartily wish that conjecture about Emily's lovers might cease as unprofitable. Of course her poems are all "fragments of a great confession": of course she wrote out of her life, her life on various levels. But books on who her "lover" was turn attention from the poems to the poet, and substitute detective work for criticism. Her readers of the 1890s did not require to know what "who" or "whos" gave her insight into love and renunciation, nor need we.

It is when the best of philosophers make blunders not inherent in their systems but extraneous to it—when Berkeley, in his neo-Platonic *Siris,* advocates the panacea of tar water—that we legitimately seek a biographical explanation. And when a good poet writes inferior poems we are concerned with the reason for the badness, in order to leave, inviolate, the goodness of the other poems. But the "goodness" is not so to be explained.

One must distinguish biography from literary biography, distinguish between the study of the empirical person who wrote poems and that undeniable "personality" present in poems which makes them recognizable as written by the same person. What is biographically peculiar to the empirical person is not relevant to the "good poems," those intelligible to and valued by competent readers, which are elucidatory of our own experiences. To be sure, literary criticism can scarcely avoid a psychology of types—as it cannot dispense with a knowledge of the culture in which a poet was reared—and, certainly, cannot lack a close intimacy with the state of the language from which the poet makes artfully expressive deviations. But biographical studies and culture-history—for those who practice them, ends in themselves—are to be used by a critic with caution and delicacy. Scholarship as such restricts a great poet to her own time, place, and empirical self. Criticism must delicately "clear" the poems for present use and evaluation—show what is for our time, or, more grandiosely, what is for all times.

I make these commonplaces of neoclassical and contemporary criticism, conscious that, in what immediately follows, I may seem to diverge from them. There is a "lion in the way" of contemporary readers of Emily—the lion of biography. It has proved impossible not to pursue, to an extent, the facts gathered and the speculations offered by those who have sought to attach Emily's power as a poet of love and death to some single love and renunciation.

—Warren, Austin. "Emily Dickinson." In *Emily Dickinson: A Collection of Critical Essays,* Richard Sewall, ed. Englewood Cliffs, NJ: Prentice-Hall, Inc., 1963.

ALBERT GELPI ON SEEING "NEW ENGLANDLY": FROM EDWARDS TO EMERSON TO DICKINSON

[Albert Gelpi is professor of English at Stanford University. His best-known book is *The Tenth Muse*, a study of American poetry.]

The critic can cull the poems and letters for a catalogue of transcendental "doctrines" which the poet had, for the moment at any rate, espoused. If Emerson referred to the world as "a divine dream, from which we may presently awake," Dickinson said: "Reality is a dream from which but a portion of mankind have yet waked." If Emerson urged self-knowledge and self-reliance, Dickinson exhorted her poetic persona:

> Soto! Explore thyself!
> Therein thyself shalt find
> The "Undiscovered Continent"—
> No Settler had the Mind. (#832)

And:

> Lad of Athens, faithful be
> To Thyself,
> And Mystery—
> All the rest is Perjury— (#1768)

If Emerson perceived the correspondence which made the world the emblematic "web of God," Dickinson saw things as "trembling Emblems" and felt the movements of an unseen Weaver. If Emerson's position rested on the divine faculty of Intuition, Dickinson claimed "Glee intuitive" as "the gift of God."

Anyone who has given Emerson and Dickinson a thorough reading can indulge in the game of finding more cases in point, but such analogues could be misleading if they are insisted upon too rigidly, because the words of a lyric poet like Emily Dickinson express not philosophic generalizations but the measure of a particular moment. On the other hand, the critic cannot resign himself to an aimless chronological reading of almost 1800 lyrics. He must try to perceive in the shifting record of successive moments the salient recurrences, relations, and patterns without reducing the poet's mind to an abstraction. And so we must watch Emily approach Emerson by a dark and circuitous path.

Wherever Emily Dickinson's mental processes may have led, they began with an intolerable sense of emptiness which drove her to project as concrete evidence of her incompleteness the loss of childhood, father, mother, lover. She could list childhood and the dead among the "Things that never can come back"; she could even enumerate the things lost with childhood. But in all honesty she had to add: "But is that all I have lost—memory drapes her Lips." These losses—genuine and heartfelt—were at least definable and hence bearable, but what seemed excruciating was the fact that almost the first act of the mind was an awareness of isolation. Edwards would have attributed this knowledge to original sin, and Emerson to the separation of the object from the Oversoul. But Emily Dickinson's was a characteristically personal response: all she knew was that she had to manage somehow from day to day, eating and sleeping and speaking and acting in the hollowness of the void:

> A loss of something ever felt I—
> The first that I could recollect
> Bereft I was—of what I knew not (#959)

The poem does not specify what was lost; all she could say was that she was bereft of something in and of herself, something so private that it belonged to her as an individual and would make her, as she was not now, a whole person.

> I cannot buy it—'tis not sold—
> There is no other in the World—
> Mine was the only one. (#840)

Before anything—faith, love, happiness—were possible, before she could give or take or act, the unknown factor had somehow to be found:

> If I could find it Anywhere
> I would not mind the journey there
> Though it took all my store (#840)

So hers was a quest through an interior waste land, trackless and guideless, without even the name of the missing treasure. She could call it what she would—friend, lover, mother, father, "Golden Fleece," God—but these names could never contain the dark immensity of "Missing All." Life began with "Missing All"; and its trek through time seemed a dreary repetition of losses, of missing in turn each of the things most dear, until "Parting is all we know of heaven,/ And all we need of hell." In this private hell the lonely mourner "walked among the children."

Even Satan, however, soon found that hell had its own compensations—the stimulus to yearn and struggle and resist. And in her own way Emily Dickinson came to draw sustenance from the substance of her sorrow. "I always try to think in any disappointment that had I been gratified, it had been sadder still, and I weave from such suppositions, at times, considerable consolation; consolation upside down as I am pleased to call it." "Consolation upside down" gave way sometimes to a brighter possibility: "To miss you, Sue, is power"; "Possession— has a sweeter chink/ Upon a Miser's Bar." Nor was she seeking solace in futile paradox; she was stating, flatly, and deliberately, her recognition of the only grounds on which life without delusion was possible: "The stimulus of Loss makes most Possession mean."

—Gelpi, Albert. "Seeing New Englandly: From Edwards to Emerson to Dickinson." In *Emily Dickinson: The Mind of the Poet*. Cambridge, MA: Harvard University Press, 1966.

Joanne Feit Diehl on Emerson, Dickinson, and the Abyss

[Joanne Feit Diehl teaches English and American Literature at the University of California, Davis, and is the author of *Dickinson and the Romantic Imagination*.]

Arachne, maiden of legendary audacity, claimed she could weave more splendidly than the goddess Minerva herself; the challenge ended in self-inflicted death and metamorphosis into a spider—the cunning revenge of the Divine weaver. Dickinson betrays a similar boldness, placing her poems against the most powerful voices of her generation—the poets of Romanticism. Like the Romantics, she writes quest poems, for they seek to complete the voyage, to prove the strength of the imagination against the stubbornness of life, the repression of an antithetical nature, and that "hidden mystery," the final territory of death. The form of the poems reflects their subject. She writes poems of "radical inquiry," riddles that tease the intelligence or alternatively achieve startling definitions which testify to the authority of her own consciousness. Such authority depends on power, and it is power that lies at the center of Dickinson's relation to Emerson. It is from Emerson that she learns the terms of the struggle and what she needs to conquer—to write poems that win from nature the triumph of freedom for the imagination.

Each of us holds a particular, if hidden, resentment towards the voice that first liberates us. How strong the antagonistic joy for Dickinson to read, almost in "credo" form, a validation of her initial aims in Emerson's essay, "The Poet"! The controlling image of poet as reader of the universe leads to his observing minute particulars, studying his relation to the text, his subject-symbol, finding what will suffice as an adequate symbol for the self. The poet must be more than a scrupulous reader, for "there is no fact in nature which does not carry the whole sense of nature," and even he is part of the process itself: "We are symbols and inhabit symbols." To carry the creative emphasis further, the "poet is the Namer or Language-maker." In conclusion, all is in nature, and the force of the poet's imagination determines his success in hearing and reading the natural world. Emerson had yet to learn, in 1842, what he knew later—that such certain knowledge, a complete ability to read a text, was beyond any human poet. In "Experience," Emerson was to envision both life and the man living it as the result of illusions. The individual is limited to creating the illusion determined by his own qualities; we are left with the power to live within our self-created deceptions: "Dream delivers us to dream, and there is no end to illusion. . . . We animate what we can, and we see only what we animate. Nature and books belong to the eyes that see them." And, a little later in the essay, Emerson emphasizes the negative aspects of this personal dream: "Temperament also enters fully into the system of illusions and shuts us in a prison of glass which we cannot see."

In response to the Emerson of "The Poet," Dickinson works out her own solution as she asserts that nature is not the sacred text, ready to reveal all if we read it right. She contends not only that we can never attain to full knowledge of nature, that our view is dominated by our eye; she extends the negative cast of Emerson's opening pages of "Illusions": "There is illusion that shall deceive even the elect. There is illusion that shall deceive even the performer of the miracle. Though he make his body, he denies it." For her, nature becomes an antagonist, a deeply equivocal mystery, certainly exquisite at times, but with an exotic power that withholds its secrets as it dazzles. No matter how well one reads or imagines, nature as text withdraws and guards its final lesson; morality departs from the natural world to depend solely upon the individual. Consequently, the self perceives nature as an adversary and seeks to go beyond it into an anti- or post-naturalistic environment, pursuing questions in a self-dominated sphere that rejects the province of a communal, natural life.

—Diehl, Joanne Feit. "Emerson, Dickinson, and the Abyss." In *Dickinson and the Romantic Imagination*. Princeton: Princeton University Press, 1981.

CHARLES R. ANDERSON ON DESPAIR

[Charles R. Anderson retired in 1969 as Caroline Donovan Professor of English at Johns Hopkins University. Besides his work on Dickinson, he is known for his writings on Melville, Thoreau, and Henry James.]

Anguish confined entirely to this world can be devastating enough, by reason of its very intensity. It is aggravated by the realization that man can find no help for it outside himself, as he can with spiritual despair through the hope of God's grace. Contrary to many of the romantic poets who preceded her, she found no healing balm in nature for human hurt. The absolute cleavage between man and the external world was one of her basic convictions . . . and its indifference to his plight is the theme-song in many of her poems. Her best one on the theme of human suffering confronted by nature's gay parade seems on the surface to be in danger of a reverse use of the pathetic fallacy, for here the indifference is threatening at several points to break out into open hostility, but a close reading proves she has not lapsed into the error of making nature sentient. On the contrary, she has made deliberate use of emotional extravagance to create a sense of nightmare, such as might result when anguish had reduced its victim to irrational terror:

I dreaded that first Robin, so,
But He is mastered, now.
I'm some accustomed to Him grown,
He hurts a little, though—

I thought if I could only live
Till that first Shout got by—
Not all Pianos in the Woods
Had power to mangle me—

I dared not meet the Daffodils—
For fear their Yellow Gown
Would pierce me with a fashion
So foreign to my own—

I wished the Grass would hurry
So—when 'twas time to see—
He'd be too tall, the tallest one
Could stretch—to look at me—

I could not bear the Bees should come,
I wished they'd stay away
In those dim countries where they go,
What word had they, for me?

They're here, though; not a creature failed—
No Blossom stayed away
In gentle deference to me—
The Queen of Calvary—

Each one salutes me, as he goes,
And I my childish Plumes,
Life, in bereaved acknowledgement
Of their unthinking Drums— (#348)

She feared the sounds of spring would 'mangle' her, its colors 'pierce' her, and so on. Nature is not only personified but on the warpath, the poet's soul so hypersensitive it can be wounded by anything, her emotions exaggerated to the point of being ludicrous. These certainly seem like the signposts of sentimentalism, and the casual reader may easily misinterpret them. Aware she was using a precarious technique, she matched her skill to the risk. The overwrought center is deftly set apart by being related in the past tense and is provided with a frame of irony by the opening and closing stanzas, which enable her and the reader to view it objectively from the calmer present. The nightmare is confined to stanzas two through five. They record not what actually happened but what she 'dreaded' would happen. The past tense, and the subjunctive mood, shows that for this part of the story's enactment spring had not yet come; the section opens with the clue 'I thought if I could only live/ Till. . . . ' The events that follow never existed anywhere except in her deluded imagination, but in that interior world they constituted the whole of reality and they function with terrifying precision. For an adult to hide behind grass blades for protection against the spears of attacking daffodils would indeed be insane, but that is just the point. This and the other imagined events are paranoid images skillfully objectifying the hallucinatory world of her fears.

The initial image sets the tone by evoking the exact sense of unreality desired: 'Not all Pianos in the Woods/Had power to mangle me.' In one sense 'Pianos' is a metaphor for the treble of birds, the bass of frogs, and all the range of natural sounds in between, with their wild harmony and counterpoint. In a letter to Higginson she once said, 'the noise in the Pool, at Noon—excels my Piano.' In a lesser poem on the same theme she uses a similar figure, the black birds' 'Banjo,' accurate enough for their twanging monotone and with the added humor of an oblique reference to the Negro minstrels popular in that day. But the humor appropriate to anguish is macabre, not grotesque, and the 'Pianos' here give just that touch. For in another sense they are not metaphorical but real, or rather surrealistic, like the objects in a painting by Dali. Placed in the woods instead of in the parlor, by the distortion of terror, they could become instruments of torture. Caught behind the keyboard of a gigantic piano she would be 'mangled' by its hammers even as she was driven mad by the booming strings, helplessly dodging blows whose source, timing, and spacing she could not guess. This is indeed the world of nightmare, induced by dread when unbearable pain has unhinged the reason. . . .

To the readiest cliché of both the sentimentalist and the pragmatist, that 'Time assuages,' she replied, not when it is 'Malady'; and in a letter: 'to all except anguish, the mind soon adjusts.' Extreme suffering even changes the very nature of time, she demonstrated in a pair of dialectical quatrains: 'Pain—expands the Time— . . . Pain contracts—the Time.' It makes clock and calendar meaningless and annihilates the very idea of eternity; the true center of pain exists in a temporal vacuum, containing its own past and future. Spatially it is equally limitless and without definable locality: it 'ranges Boundlessness.' Unlike contentment, which resides lawfully in a 'quiet Suburb,' agony cannot stay 'In Acre—Or Location—/It rents Immensity.' It absorbs the whole of consciousness, condensed to a measureless, momentless point.

Pain is thus a quality of being that exists outside time and space, the only two terms in which it can possibly be externalized. Her dilemma in describing this formless psychic entity was how to contrive outward symbols that would make the internal condition manifest. In solving this difficulty she borrowed from the techniques of the theatre, man's supreme contrivance for presenting illusion by making scene and action a set of appearances through which the spectator must penetrate to the reality beneath. With the aid of this device, supplemented by the rituals of formal ceremonies like trials and funerals, the effects of extreme pain are rendered by her in a series of unusually interesting poems.

In the most extraordinary of them, the abstract concept of 'death' as inflicted on the consciousness by despair is projected in one of those courtroom scenes of nightmare made vivid to modern readers by Kafka. The victim is on trial for his life, though for some nameless crime, and the machinery of an inexorable justice grinds to its conclusion, without moving, in a kind of wordless horror:

> I read my sentence—steadily—
> Reviewed it with my eyes,
> To see that I made no mistake
> In its extremest clause—
> The Date, and manner, of the shame—
> And then the Pious Form
> That 'God have mercy' on the Soul
> The Jury voted Him—
> I made my soul familiar—with her extremity—
> That at the last, it should not be a novel Agony—
> But she, and Death, acquainted—
> Meet tranquilly, as friends—
> Salute, and pass, without a Hint—
> And there, the Matter ends— (#412)

The proliferation of pronouns here is not a sign of artistic confusion but a grammatical echo of the dream chaos, whose intricate meaning can be parsed readily enough if the analyst follows the mode of the subconscious drama. 'I,' 'Him,' and 'She' are all aspects of the persona of the poem, as in the dream all characters are projections of the dreamer.

—Anderson, Charles R. "Despair." In *Emily Dickinson's Poetry: Stairway of Surprise.* New York: Holt, Rinehart and Winston, 1960.

CRISTANNE MILLER ON EMERSON'S THEORIES OF LANGUAGE

[Cristanne Miller is professor of English at Pomona College, author of *Emily Dickinson: A Poet's Grammar,* and coauthor (with Suzanne Juhasz and Martha Nell Smith) of *Comic Power in Emily Dickinson.*]

To the extent that language does reflect the world for Dickinson, her conception of language is closer to Emerson's than to the Puritans'. The Amherst poet was familiar with the Concord poet's works from at least 1850 on. In that year, she received "a beautiful copy" of Emerson's 1847 *Poems.* In 1857 Emerson lectured in Amherst, eating and sleeping at the Evergreens, where Emily may have joined Austin and Sue in entertaining him. She told Sue that he seemed "as if he had come from where dreams are born." In 1876 the poet gave Mrs. Higginson a copy of *Representative Men*—"a little Granite Book you can lean upon." She also quotes or paraphrases five of Emerson's poems in her letters and poems, most notably his "Bacchus" in her "I taste a liquor never brewed" (#214) and "The Snow Storm" in her "It sifts from Leaden Sieves" (#311).

Emerson writes at length of language as an ideal system of meaning in his essays "Nature" and "The Poet." His use of language in his own prose, however, contradicts his theories. In theory, Emerson's notion of language stems from Puritan ideas of the word as an extension of the Oversoul, or God. For him, as for the Puritans, language in its pristine or original state is transparent: "Words are signs of natural facts." Similarly, for Emerson, speech that derives from an accurate perception of nature "is at once a commanding certificate that he who employs it is a man in alliance with truth and God." In its ideal form, language translates and interprets spiritual truths as for the Puritans, but now through the mediation of nature. Because of this mediation, at its plainest and most authoritative language is "picturesque"; it is "poetry." Words stand for (name, signify) facts of nature, which are in turn "emblematic" of spiritual facts. Language, then, is both referential (transparently reflective of nature) and metaphorical. Human language derives from nature, which is in turn "the organ through which the universal spirit speaks to the individual." Ideally there would be a one-to-one correspondence between the facts of nature, the words of speech, and the facts of the spirit; that is, human language would exactly reproduce the language of the universe.

Because of its base in nature, according to Emerson, language is also both fixed or universal and constantly undergoing change. The laws of the spirit or Oversoul, the ultimate referent of language, do not change, but their forms in nature may. Natural objects "furnish man with the dictionary and grammar of his municipal speech"; when these objects are altered so are the meanings of our language. Each age requires its own interpreter or poet to keep language true to nature (and to read nature's new forms) but each interpreter expresses the same truths, albeit in different forms. Because the laws of nature are fixed, the primary act of language making is naming and the principle word is the noun. Emerson traces the development of language through that of the individual: "Children and savages use only nouns or names of things, which they convert into verbs and apply to analogous mental acts"—a necessary stage in language-making, he implies, but a departure from language as pure poetry. Verbs provide, as it were, the transitional form in the desired transformation of language from directly referential (noun to fact) to symbolic (noun to spiritual fact). Language translates perceived nature into human speech and thereby assists in the transformation of nature into spirit. It is not itself stable, but it leads from the world of nameable things to the sphere of immutable spirit.

Emerson never develops the implications of this philosophy for the use of a particular syntax or parts of speech. Were he to do so, the poet or premier language user would logically be Adamic, a pronouncer of names. The ceaseless contradictions and qualifications of Emerson's prose, however, suggest otherwise. Although he preaches about natural laws, he sees nothing but change, and he bases all knowledge and all language on what may be seen (the inner eye interpreting through the outer. While at one minute in "Self-Reliance" he commandingly and absolutely propounds: "Trust thyself: every heart vibrates to that iron string" or "Whoso would be a man must be a nonconformist," in the next he questions: "Suppose you should contradict yourself; what then?" In a longer passage from the same essay, Emerson characteristically combines highly embedded syntax replete with parallel modifiers and self-referring phrases with paratactically juxtaposed aphorisms as pithy as any that Dickinson coins: "In this pleasing contrite wood-life which God allows me, let me record day by day my honest thought without prospect or retrospect, and, I cannot doubt, it will be found symmetrical though I mean it not and see it not. My book should smell of pines and resound with the hum of insects. The swallow over my window should interweave that thread or straw he carries in his bill into my web also. We pass for what we are. Character teaches above our wills." Emerson's essays move by associative elaboration of a central idea—often first presented in metaphorical form—not by formal, logical stages or steps. He uses language as if its meaning were less certain or clear than he describes it as being.

—Miller, Cristanne. "Emerson's Theories of Language." In *Emily Dickinson: A Poet's Grammar.* Cambridge, MA: Harvard University Press, 1989.

SUZANNE JUHASZ ON THE LANDSCAPE OF THE SPIRIT

[Suzanne Juhasz is professor of English at the University of Colorado, Boulder, and editor of *The Emily Dickinson Journal.* Her books include *The Undiscovered Continent: Emily Dickinson and the Space of the Mind, Comic Power in Emily Dickinson* (with Cristanne Miller and Martha Nell Smith), and *Reading from the Heart: Women, Literature, and the Search for True Love.*]

Nevertheless, Dickinson was attracted to people, men and women. Her friendships were never casual. Her letters as well as her poems, written to the friends of her girlhood, to male friends both identified and unidentified, to older women and younger nieces, all show how overwhelmingly significant those she loved were to her. Love itself was for her an essential, and consuming, emotion. She did not choose not to marry and bear children because she could not, or would not, love. Her choice seems to have had more to do with her greater need to maintain herself and also with the ways in which she did experience love. Sewall comments on her friendships as follows: "All her life she demanded too much of people. Her early girlfriends could hardly keep up with her tumultuous letters or, like Sue, could not or would not take her into their lives as she wanted to be taken. They had other concerns. The young men, save for a few who had amusing or edifying intellectual exchanges with her, apparently shied away. Eliza Coleman's fear that her friends in Amherst 'wholly misinterpret' her, was a polite way of saying, perhaps, that they would not respond with the intensity she apparently demanded of everyone." Sewall continues: "meetings themselves became ordeals . . . in her own economy, she found that she had to ration them very carefully."

Given her propensity for passions more intense than their recipients could return, Dickinson used physical distance, and language, to deal with love. "After you went," she wrote to her friend Mrs. Holland, "a low wind warbled through the house like a spacious bird, making it high but lonely. When you had gone the love came. I supposed it would. The supper of the heart is when the guest has gone."

Thus, because of her own temperament, her intensity and sensitivity; because of her ambitions for herself, her stubborn dedication to her sense of vocation; because of her situation as a woman in middle-class Amherst society in nineteenth-century America with its expectations for normal womanhood; Emily Dickinson, a woman who wanted to be a poet, chose to withdraw from the external world and to live her most significant life in the world of her mind. This decision was surely what enabled her to be the poet that she became. It gave her control over her own experience: she could select, apportion, focus, examine, explore, satiate herself exactly as she wished and needed to do, such that poetry could result. In the outer world, this manner of control would have been impossible. It gave her, as well, the possibility for complete and thorough experience, for risk, intensity, range, and depth, that as a woman she could never have achieved in the world at large. She could not wander across the continent, like Walt Whitman; but she could move freely in the "undiscovered continent," the mind.

Such a description of mental experience assumes, categorically, that these events are real. Even as Dickinson wishes to think of the mind itself as actual space, so she is insistent throughout her poetry that mental experience is in no way less real than what happens in the world outside. When David Porter writes of Dickinson's poems, "There is no final reality, and the loss of that reality is a function of a language intent on saying itself and not on signifying a specific world," or, "Dickinson had no subject, least of all reality," he is using a definition of reality that is based upon what he calls "the things outside her window," one which does not include in its domain mental experience. This approach does a profound disservice to the poetry. Dickinson did write, because its subject is so often exactly that: what happens in the mind.

What happens in the mind is also the subject of this book. It is common enough to hear, of Emily Dickinson's life, that "nothing happened to her." "Nothing," in fact, tends to happen to most women, because, as we know, patriarchal history has a propensity for cataloguing battles and not dinner parties. Feminist history has begun to write the events of women's lives and call them real—not only their battle to get the vote but their daily domestic occurrences. Yet Dickinson's most important life took place not when she was baking the family's bread, but when she was adventuring dangerously and alone, in the very deep and very wide terrain of her mind: having experiences so profound and powerful that they could be the subject of great poetry. For Dickinson did not choose to be a "normal" woman, even as she did not try to pretend that she was a man. She did not choose to live where men live, in the public world, or where women live, in the domestic world. She found another place, at once more private and expansive than either of those others: the mind.

And yet I do not think that Dickinson was the first woman to discover the mind's potential as a place particularly suited for significant experience. As Patricia Meyer Spacks writes in her study of the female imagination. "The cliché that women, more consistently than men, turn inward for sustenance seems to mean, in practice, that women have richly defined the ways in which imagination creates possibility: possibility that society denies . . . women dominate their own experience by imagining it, giving it form, writing about it."

To live in the mind, an actual and occupied place, was for Dickinson the key to solving the problem of how to be a poet, of how to achieve the self-knowledge, the self-awareness, the self-fulfillment that her vocation demanded. Certainly Dickinson's tactics were extreme; but then, they were more successful than moderation might have brought. She became an extraordinary poet, as few women before or since have done. Nevertheless, I think that Dickinson was capitalizing upon a technique that women have always known and used, for survival, using the imagination as a space in which to create some life other than their external situation. What Dickinson did was to make art from it. . . .

Dickinson's poems frequently assert her sense of the mind's actuality with images of caverns and corridors (#777, #670), windows and doors (#303, #657), even cellars (#1182). Because she took the mind to be her dwelling place, it is appropriate that she use these domestic figurative correspondences to describe it. Yet her poems using such architectural analogues go beyond pointing out how a mind might be like a house. They set out to show, as well, what happens in a mind that is as a house, so that the solidity which door and window frame provide grants substance both to the setting and to the events occurring within. The architectural vocabulary usually portrays the mind as an enclosed space, its confinement responsible for power, safety, yet fearful confrontation.

Poem #303 is a strong statement about the power of the self alone. The soul is shown living within a space defined by door, gate, and mat. The external world, with its nations and their rulers, is kept outside.

> The Soul selects her own Society—
> Then—shuts the Door—
> To her divine Majority—
> Present no more—
>
> Unmoved—she notes the Chariots—pausing—
> At her low Gate—
> Unmoved—an Emperor be kneeling
> Upon her Mat—

> I've known her—from an ample nation—
> Choose One—
> Then—close the Valves of her attention—
> Like Stone—

Traditional ideas about power are reversed here. Not control over vast populations but the ability to construct a world for oneself comprises the greatest power, a god-like achievement, announces the opening stanza. Not only is the soul alone "divine," but it is also identified as "Society" and "Majority": the poem also challenges our ideas about what constitutes a social group. Consequently, the enclosed space of the soul's house is more than adequate for a queenly life, and ambassadors of the external world's glories, even emperors, can easily be scorned. Yet while the speaker claims her equality with those most powerful in the outer world—they may be emperors, but she is "divine Majority," at the same time she asserts her difference from them; for her domestic vocabulary of door, low gate, and mat establishes her dwelling as not a grand palace but rather a simple house.

—Juhasz, Suzanne. "The Landscape of the Spirit." In *Emily Dickinson: A Collection of Critical Essays,* Judith Farr, ed. Upper Saddle River, NJ: Prentice Hall, 1990.

CRISTANNE MILLER ON THE CONSENT OF LANGUAGE AND THE WOMAN POET

[Cristanne Miller is professor of English at Pomona College, author of *Emily Dickinson: A Poet's Grammar*, and coauthor (with Suzanne Juhasz and Martha Nell Smith) of *Comic Power in Emily Dickinson.*]

Even human language is more useful than God's Word and therefore to be preferred, despite the clear advantages that the absolute creativity and power of the latter would bring. Dickinson begins the following poem with a celebration of language's power generally and with reverberating religious connotation ("A Word made Flesh is seldom/And tremblingly partook"), but ends by contrasting God's Word, Christ, with human "Philology":

> A Word that breathes distinctly
> Has not the power to die
> Cohesive as the Spirit
> It may expire if He—
> "Made Flesh and dwelt among us"
> Could condescension be
> Like this consent of Language
> This loved Philology. (#1651)

Here again the conditional "Could" calls into question whether divine language is capable of the service human language routinely performs. In "condescension" Dickinson plays on the words "descend," as the Spirit did in the form of a dove at Christ's baptism, and "condescend," with its glance at what may be either God's benign courtesy or His hierarchical system that keeps humanity low. Contrasting God's "condescension" with philology's "consent," the poet appears to say that the ability to expire—breathe as well as die—is crucial in language and perhaps inseparable from its relation to human need and use. God's Word cannot die, but neither, apparently, can it live with us.

The human word, in contrast, is represented by "Philology," by human response (love and study) to language's power rather than by authoritative creation or Adamic naming. Philology represents an exchange between speakers and the categorizable aspects of language, which is valued for its complexity and for its dependence on those to whom it "consents." In this poem human language is twice "loved" (in the adjective and, etymologically, in *philo-logos*) because it communicates *with* us; it consents to our manipulation, which in turn replenishes its meaning. As Dickinson says in another poem, a word "just/Begins to live" when it is spoken (#1212). As letter writer, as daughter, sister, and friend as well as in the personae of her poems, Dickinson is a poet of "consent," of the shifting transformation rather than the authoritative establishment of meaning.

The cooperation of language is clearly necessary for such a poet, and perhaps for any poet. Curiously, however, most of Dickinson's poems on poetry are more about the conditions the poet must suffer or overcome than about language or the poet's aesthetic choices; the speaker is only metaphorically a poet. Through their repeated emphasis on the need for escape, or opposition, or defensive contrast of the poet's work with that of some greater or more public figure, these poems define poetry as an aggressive act of expression rather than as an icon or publicly valued art. The speaker's attitude toward her audience often resembles that of the speaker toward God in the poems just quoted, and her metaphorical creation is the method of her rebellion or escape. In some poems, the two types of authority are combined and the poet/speaker stands in opposition to God, as in "Why—do they shut Me out of Heaven?" (#248), or "A Word made Flesh is seldom" (#1651), or in the ugly-duckling tale "God made a little Gentian," where the poet suddenly makes herself analogous to the ravishing late bloomer and ambiguously threatens: "Creator—Shall I—bloom?" (#442). In "I reckon—when I count at all" (#569), the speaker claims to value poets, the sun, summer, and "the Heaven of God—", then decides that poets "Comprehend the Whole—" and chooses their rewards over any others, especially over God's.

—Miller, Cristanne. "The Consent of Language and the Woman Poet." In *Emily Dickinson: A Poet's Grammar*. Cambridge, MA: Harvard University Press, 1989.

Thematic Analysis of
"Because I could not stop for Death" (#712)

This is perhaps Emily Dickinson's best-known poem. She personifies the character of death and then dramatizes the experience: Death is portrayed as a genteel friend who "kindly" stops to take her to her grave. Death is an entity, as distinguished from the moment of death itself. She separates Death from Immortality, whom she represents as a fellow passenger on her journey.

A certain emotional detachment here allows Dickinson some levity, a mood not often associated with her poetry. The scene certainly is not one of despair: two men and a woman are being driven on a leisurely ride in a carriage. The meter and rhyme are also uncharacteristically balanced and uniform, with even, iambic lines. The journey takes her past a review of her life. At the school, she sees children at play. Passing fields of grain, she is made aware of the fullness of life. As the sun sets, she senses her life drawing to a close and a chill overtakes her; her gown is thin and gossamer and can protect her no longer. Then Death pauses, allowing her to view her own grave, "A Swelling of the Ground," her new home. The image here of a woman and her escort, Death, meditating on the prospect of eternity, is neither one of despair nor loss nor outrage, but of resignation.

In another poem about death, #465, Dickinson re-creates the drama of the deathbed. The central character is a fly, whose buzzing interrupts and exaggerates the silence of the scene—no shock, no sorrow, no desperation. The poem communicates the profundity of the experience through stillness and absence.

> I heard a Fly buzz—when I died—
> The Stillness in the Room
> Was like the Stillness in the Air—
> Between the Heaves of Storm—
>
> The Eyes around—had wrung them dry—
> And Breaths were gathering firm
> For that last Onset—when the King
> Be witnessed—in the Room—
>
> I willed my Keepsakes—Signed away
> What portion of me be

Assignable—and then it was
There interposed a Fly—

With Blue—uncertain stumbling Buzz—
Between the light—and me—
And then the Windows failed—and then
I could not see to see—

As in "Because I could not stop for Death," the poet's declarations
are limited to the pronoun "I." The word "I," in fact, appears more
frequently in Dickinson's poetry than any other word, bearing marks
of the biblical "I say unto you." Although wary of Puritanical didacti-
cism, and skeptical of Christianity, her interest in religion nevertheless does not diminish. Rarely alluding to the stories in the Bible,
except humorously, she employs biblical imagery, in effect assimi-
lating it in order to supplant it. Dickinson divides herself from the
fictive "I," using it to mediate and translate moments of vision—the
volcanic eruptions—that become her poetry. The truth, her Truth, is
informed by the "Soul's Superior instants" (#306). When Dickinson
declares her "I," these instants become our own.

Her rigorous, flinty honesty permits her to explore the abyss that
for her is not death but despair. Greater than death, despair is a paradoxical experience, including glimmers of a kind of ecstasy. Death,
on the other hand, is slower and more restrained—a gentleman in a
carriage, a pleasant ride in the country.

The will to live in the face of death—and the joy this will creates—is a theme in many of Dickinson's poems, particularly this
one, and is remarkably modern. Emerson, her contemporary and
inspiration, would have found her stance morbid if not intolerable.
Emerson and the nineteenth-century Romantics believed in the triumph of transcendental man—a being without bounds, inseparable
from nature, which is to say, from the divine; for them, man is not
impotent but is caught "within the circuit of this plodding life"
(#670). For Dickinson, the moment of divine, pure wisdom comes
with the acceptance of loss and defeat.

We must be able to see in order for God to become visible. Our
souls must emerge to face the light of God. In these visionary
moments, we become like "Holy Ghosts in cages."

The Music in the Violin
Does not emerge alone
But Arm in Arm with Touch, yet Touch
Alone—is not a Tune—
The Spirit lurks within the Flesh
Like Tides within the Sea
That make the Water live, estranged
What would the Either be? (#1576)

Heaven plays no part in "Because I could not stop for Death." Eternity is achieved here through the visionary moment, which exists outside space and time. Dickinson's heaven is an earth-heaven; it is the intensity of our lives fully lived that offers paradise. Although the inevitability of death makes life far from perfect, death is necessary: Death concentrates life, formulating its transcendent essence. This is the essence for which Dickinson struggled in her poetry.

Essential Oils—are wrung—
The Attar from the Rose
Be not expressed by Suns—alone—
It is the gift of Screws— (#675)

Perfume emerges from the rose through a process involving screws, not by natural growth. That perfume outlasts the flower, the maker, and even the wearer. ❀

Critical Views on
"Because I could not stop for Death" (#712)

ALLEN TATE ON EMILY DICKINSON

[Allen Tate, professor of English at the University of Minnesota, is a novelist, critic, and poet.]

One of the better poems in English is "The Chariot," and it illustrates better than anything else she wrote the special quality of her mind. I think it will illuminate the tendency of this discussion:

> Because I could not stop for death,
> He kindly stopped for me;
> The carriage held but just ourselves
> And immortality.
>
> We slowly drove, he knew no haste,
> And I had put away
> My labor, and my leisure too,
> For his civility.
>
> We passed the school where children played,
> Their lessons scarcely done;
> We passed the fields of gazing grain,
> We passed the setting sun.
>
> We paused before a house that seemed
> A swelling of the ground;
> The roof was scarcely visible,
> The cornice but a mound.
>
> Since then 'tis centuries; but each
> Feels shorter than the day
> I first surmised the horses' heads
> Were toward eternity.

If the word "great" means anything in poetry, this poem is one of the greatest in the English language. The rhythm charges with movement the pattern of suspended action back of the poem. Every image is precise and, moreover, not merely beautiful, but fused with the central idea. Every image extends and intensifies every other. The third stanza especially shows Miss Dickinson's power to fuse, into a single order of perception, a heterogeneous series: the children, the grain, and the setting sun (time) have the same degree of credibility; the first subtly preparing for the last. The sharp gazing before grain instills into nature a cold vitality of which the qualitative richness has infinite depth. The content of death in the poem eludes explicit definition. He is a gentleman taking a lady out for a drive. But note the restraint that keeps the poet from carrying this so far that it becomes ludicrous and incredible; and note the subtly interfused erotic motive, which the idea of death has presented to most romantic poets, love being a symbol interchangeable with death. The terror of death is objectified through this figure of the genteel driver, who is made ironically to serve the end of Immortality. This is the heart of the poem: she has presented a typical Christian theme in its final irresolution, without making any final statements about it. There is no solution to the problem; there can be only a presentation of it in the full context of intellect and feeling. A construction of the human will, elaborated with all the abstracting powers of the mind, is put to the concrete test of experience: the idea of immortality is confronted with the fact of physical disintegration. We are not told what to think; we are told to look at the situation.

The framework of the poem is, in fact, the two abstractions, mortality and eternity, which are made to associate in equality with the images: she sees the ideas, and thinks the perceptions. She did, of course, nothing of the sort; but we must use the logical distinctions, even to the extent of paradox, if we are to form any notion of this rare quality of mind. She could not in the proper sense think at all, and unless we prefer the feeble poetry of moral ideas that flourished in New England in the eighties, we must conclude that her intellectual deficiency contributed at least negatively to her great distinction. Miss Dickinson is probably the only Anglo-American poet of her century whose work exhibits the perfect literary situation—in which is possible the fusion of sensibility and thought. Unlike her contemporaries, she never succumbed to her ideas, to easy solutions, to her private desires.

—Tate, Allen. "Emily Dickinson." In *Collected Essays*. Denver: The Swallow Press, 1932.

YVOR WINTERS ON EMILY DICKINSON AND THE LIMITS OF JUDGMENT

[Yvor Winters, professor of English at Stanford University, has published *In Defense of Reason* and *The Poetry of W. B. Yeats*.]

There are a few curious and remarkable poems representing a mixed theme, of which the following is perhaps the finest example.

> Because I could not stop for death,
> He kindly stopped for me;
> The carriage held but just ourselves
> And Immortality.
>
> We slowly drove, he knew no haste,
> And I had put away
> My labor, and my leisure too,
> For his civility.
>
> We passed the school where children played,
> Their lessons scarcely done;
> We passed the fields of gazing grain,
> We passed the setting sun.
>
> We paused before a house that seemed
> A swelling of the ground;
> The roof was scarcely visible,
> The cornice but a mound.
>
> Since then 'tis centuries; but each
> Feels shorter than the day
> I first surmised the horses' heads
> Were toward eternity.

In the fourth line we find the familiar device of using a major abstraction in a somewhat loose and indefinable manner; in the last stanza there is the semi-playful pretence of familiarity with the posthumous experience of eternity, so that the poem ends unconvincingly though gracefully, with a formulary gesture very roughly comparable to that of the concluding couplet of many an Elizabethan sonnet of love; for the rest the poem is a remarkably beautiful poem on the subject of the daily realization of the imminence of death—it is a poem of departure from life, an intensely conscious leave-taking. In so far as it concentrates on the life that is being left behind, it is wholly successful; in so far as it attempts to experience the death to come, it is fraudulent, however exquisitely, and in this it falls below her finest achievement. Allen Tate, who appears to be unconcerned with this fraudulent element, praises the poem in the highest terms; he appears almost to praise it for its defects: "The sharp *gazing* before *grain* instills into nature a kind of cold vitality of which the qualitative richness has infinite depth. The content of death in the poem eludes forever any explicit definition . . . she has presented a typical Christian theme in all its final irresolution, without making any final statement about it." The poem ends in irresolution in the sense that it ends in a statement that is not offered seriously; to praise the poem for this is unsound criticism, however. It is possible to solve any problem of insoluble experience by retreating a step and defining the boundary at which comprehension ceases, and by then making the necessary moral adjustments to that boundary; this in itself is an experience both final and serious, and it is the experience on which our author's finest work is based.

Let me illustrate by citation. The following poem defines the subject which the mystical poems endeavor to conceal: the soul is taken to the brink of the incomprehensible, and is left there, for retreat is impossible, and advance is impossible without a transmutation of the soul's very nature. The third and fourth lines display the playful redundancy of her weaker poems, but the intrusion of the quality here is the result of habit, and is a minor defect; there is nothing in the conception of the poem demanding a compromise. There is great power in the phrasing of the remainder of the poem, especially the middle stanza:

> Our journey had advanced;
> Our feet were almost come
> To that odd fork in Being's road,
> Eternity by term.
>
> Our pace took sudden awe,
> Our feet reluctant led.
> Before were cities, but between
> The forest of the dead.
>
> Retreat was out of hope,—
> Behind, a sealëd route,
> Eternity's white flag before,
> And God at every gate.

She is constantly defining the absolute cleavage between the living and the dead.

—Winters, Yvor. "Emily Dickinson and the Limits of Judgment." In *In Defense of Reason*. Denver: The Swallow Press, 1938.

GEORGE F. WHICHER ON AMERICAN HUMOR

[George F. Whicher, author of *This Was a Poet: A Critical Biography of Emily Dickinson*, also edited *Poetry of the New England Renaissance, 1790–1890*.]

The habit of combining small and great was ingrained in Emily Dickinson to such an extent that she instinctively employed it again and again in her most serious poems. When, reversing the humorous device of using the grand to express the trivial, she projected a tremendous meaning into a homely image, she not infrequently laid herself open to the suspicion of making light of sacred things or of sporting with tender feelings. But in all probability she had no thought of being flippant. A way of speaking that might afford amusement if applied to light or indifferent subjects remained her constant manner even when she dealt with her most piercing memories and profound reflections. She was able to separate any circumstance or idea at will from the sentiment normally attached to it, and thus make available for artistic use what otherwise would shock or dazzle the mind into inarticulateness.

This power of detachment, this sense of doubleness, originally fostered by the Puritan genius for introspection, was confirmed by her early saturation in humor of the frontier type. "We make a thing humorous," says Professor Cazamian, "by expressing it with a certain twist, a queer reserve, an inappropriateness, and as it were an unconsciousness of what we all the time feel it to be." This is a perfect description of the quality that Emily acquired and practiced. For the joke's sake she learned to resist the impulses of sentiment as completely as Mark Twain himself. The professional imperviousness to normal feeling evident in some of his journalistic sketches, as for example in "Cannibalism in the Cars," and in the jocular treatment of horror in general may be paralleled by bits of ruthless comedy scattered through her letters:

> Who writes those funny accidents, where railroads meet each other unexpectedly, and gentlemen in factories get their heads cut off quite informally? The author, too, relates them in such a sprightly way, that they are quite attractive. Vinnie was disappointed to-night, that there were not more accidents—I read the news aloud while Vinnie was sewing.

Add to this parlor bloodthirstiness a sample of mortuary merriment:

> No one has called so far, but one old lady to look at a house. I directed her to the cemetery to spare expense of moving.

This is a side of the sensitive and tenderly sympathetic Emily that is often overlooked. In many of her serious poems we may note a similar aloofness from the emotion implied, an odd quirk of incongruous association that in a less poignant connection we should unhesitatingly recognize as wit. It was Emily Dickinson's special faculty to stand undismayed in the midst of convulsions, some unshaken particle in her consciousness ready to note with ironical detachment the reeling of the brain.

Examples are not far to seek. If she encountered a painful disillusionment, she was as apt as not to picture it as the shattering of a dish "on the stones at bottom of my mind" (#54). The momentousness of death to her imagination did not prevent her from stating the anguish of bereavement in terms of broom and dustpan (#166):

> The sweeping up the heart,
> And putting love away
> We shall not want to use again
> Until eternity.

In a letter of 1860–61 to her Norcross cousins Emily echoed mischievously the routine question of the clerk behind the counter, "Is there nothing else?" Not long afterward, perhaps, this trite phrase blended in unexpected coalescence with her insistent cry, "Is God love's adversary?" Her frustration merged with glee as she contrived to exhibit an indifferent Providence in the figure of a village storekeeper:

The mighty merchant smiled.

Brazil? He twirled a button,
Without a glance my way:
"But, madam, is there nothing else
That we can show to-day?"

And, finally, her genuine reverence could not repress her delight
when she detected an apt metaphor for "God so loved the world that
he sent his only begotten Son" in *The Courtship of Miles Standish:*

God is a distant, stately Lover,
Woos, so He tells us, by His Son.
Surely a vicarious courtship!
Miles' and Priscilla's such a one.

—Whicher, George F. "American Humor." In *This Was a Poet.* New
York: Charles Scribner's Sons, 1938.

DAVID PORTER ON THE EARLY ACHIEVEMENT

[David Porter is professor of English at the University of
Massachusetts, Amherst. He has written *The Art of Emily
Dickinson's Early Poetry, Emerson and Literary Change,* and
Dickinson, The Modern Idiom.]

Her obsessive concern with the moment when the activity of this life
dies into soundless inactivity engendered the well-known early
poem "Safe in their Alabaster Chambers." (For analysis I use the
superior version [#216] which the poet enclosed in her first letter to
Higginson.) The work is yet another treatment of the subject of
death, of the aspiration of the dead for immortality, and of the
riddle of those that resting, rise. It possesses the characteristic
emphasis on motion and stasis which informs so much of her
poetry. Here the contrast is clearly drawn, providing the structure
for the work. Indeed, the mature artistry of the poet is evident in the
severe imagery of the stillness of the tomb in contrast to the inces-
sant motion in the universe outside. The effective force of the poem
arises from this contrast and from the brilliant closing simile in

which the motion in the second stanza is arrested in the snow image, which in turn directs the reader back again to the cold repose of the tomb with which the poem opens. Promise and denial, forever inseparable, are symbolized by the bright satin beneath the impassable stone:

> Safe in their Alabaster Chambers—
> Untouched by Morning—
> And untouched by Noon—
> Lie the meek members of the Resurrection—
> Rafter of Satin—and Roof of Stone!
>
> Grand go the Years—
> In the Crescent—above them—
> Worlds scoop their Arcs—
> And Firmaments—row—
> Diadems—drop—
> And Doges—surrender—
> Soundless as Dots—
> On a Disc of Snow—

The intrinsic control of movement within the poem yet allows an element of abiding tension created by the residual skepticism and uneasiness. For though the cycle of life is completed within the poem there is no assurance that the dead will indeed rise up to their supposed reward. They are the opposite of "grand" (as the world goes); they are "untouched" as yet by immortality. The discomfiture is sounded in the rhyme scheme, for in the opening stanza which describes the tomb where resurrection is as yet unachieved, the rhyme is only approximate. In contrast, the resolving function of the image of snow at the end is reinforced by the exact rhyme. Having encountered the apparent resolution, however, the reader is directed back by both sound and image correspondence to the opening stanza. He is turned back, that is, to the tension at the beginning. In the brief compass of thirteen lines the poet distills life and death, gathers the one into the other, leaving unresolved the promise of immortality. Elsewhere she describes this tension as

> . . . Gravity—and Expectation—and Fear—
> A tremor just, that All's not sure. (#408)

Other early poems of superior achievement cluster about the idea that the worth of an experience is ultimately best measured by those who are denied gratification in it. The central paradox is that in equal ratio to the suffering caused by denial one receives an increased comprehension.

—Porter, David. "The Early Achievement." In *The Art of Emily Dickinson's Early Poetry.* Cambridge, MA: Harvard University Press, 1966.

David Porter on Strangely Abstracted Images

[David Porter is professor of English at the University of Massachusetts, Amherst. He has written *The Art of Emily Dickinson's Early Poetry, Emerson and Literary Change,* and *Dickinson, The Modern Idiom.*]

Dickinson achieved varying degrees of success with figures made of abstractions: "Brooks of Plush—in Banks of Satin," for example, to suggest the sound of the satisfied laughter of the happy dead in their coffins (#457): "Great Streets of silence" and "Neighborhoods of Pause" for the expanse of timelessness (#1159); "a maritime conviction" for the feel of the sea in the air (#1302); the obligation/To Electricity" for the debt owed revelation (#1581). For the most part, they *mean* but do not *be.* Such resort to disembodied conceptual figures presents itself whenever we look for it in Dickinson. Two further examples, small successes of a comparable sort, though derived from different grammatical structures: "No Goblin—on the Bloom" from #646 and "no film on noon" from letter 235. Only by great transfusions of implication from their contexts does it become clear that each means there is no diminution of beauty, no apprehension, no alteration of the perfect.

The exemplar of this particular form of abstraction, now doubly deobjectified by its negative, is the image "No Furrow on the Glow" in the splendid poem of the cicada's hum, "Further in Summer than the Birds" (#1068). The last eight lines seek the instinctual sensation of seasonal change.

> Antiquest felt at Noon
> When August burning low
> Arise this spectral Canticle
> Repose to typify

Remit as yet no Grace
No Furrow on the Glow
Yet a Druidic Difference
Enhances Nature now

The image "No Furrow on the Glow" succeeds for a reader after he has known this poem a long time. Like the examples cited just previously, it similarly means there is no decline from the ideal. Specifically in this poem of high summer it means there is no evident break in summer's full brilliance (though there is simultaneously the felt turn of the season toward fall, winter, and death—which is what the poem is about). It is an idea image (what sort of furrow? what sort of glow?), Dickinson having floated out this figure as an unattached trope in free linguistic orbit.

Ezra Pound, in an essay on Cavalcanti, described a realm beyond the plastic where the poet's aesthetic requires something more than simple visual mass, not limiting itself to "the impact of light on the eye." He characterized this lost domain of Cavalcanti's as a "radiant world where one thought cuts through another with clean edge, a world of moving energies '*mezzo oscuro rade*,' '*risplende in se perpetuale effecto*,' magnetisms that take form, that are seen, or that border the visible, the matter of Dante's *paradiso*, the glass under water, the form that seems a form seen in a mirror, these realities perceptible to the sense, interacting.

Dickinson's plunge into such obscurity, which Yvor Winters cited as the source of her "nonsense," produced her drained images. To the extent they were habitual, they are radical signs of her peculiar stance before reality. A reader thus would gain valuable insight by perceiving the motion of her mind in that crucial engagement. Is it possible to be present at the making of one of those impalpable images, to locate ourselves, as Roland Barthes says, "at that very fragile and rather obscure moment when the relation of a real event is about to be apprehended by literary meaning'? There perhaps, the hidden coupling of sensation and language would be revealed. It would take us closer to the elemental act of bonding language to discrete experiences that are both inescapable and unutterable.

—Porter, David. "Strangely Abstracted Images." In *Dickinson: The Modern Idiom*. Cambridge, MA: Harvard University Press, 1981.

SHIRA WOLOSKY ON A SYNTAX OF CONTENTION

[Shira Wolosky teaches English at Yale. Her book on Dickinson is *A Voice of War.*]

She saw the end of time as providing a vantage point from which to look back on life's discrete events and in terms of which those events could be placed in sequence. They would become linked in perceivable succession, and the pattern through which each moment leads into the next would become evident. "Retrospection," she writes, "is Prospect's half" (#995). Retrospect in fact makes prospect possible. The ability to negotiate time progressively depends upon a belief that on review all the different events will be situated:

> The Admirations—and Contempts—of time—
> Show justest—through an Open Tomb—
> The Dying—as it were a Height
> Reorganizes Estimate
> And what We saw not
> We distinguish clear—
> And mostly—see not
> What We saw before—
>
> 'Tis Compound Vision—
> Light—enabling Light—
> The Finite—furnished
> With the Infinite—
> Convex—and Concave Witness—
> Back—toward Time—
> And forward—
> Toward the God of Him— (#906)

As in so many poems, Dickinson projects forward to an ultimate stance (often, as here, that of death) in order to project back to her present moment—now seen, however, from a posterior viewpoint. Dickinson, that is, would read time backwards. She attempts to establish her moments as at once viewed and reviewed. She thus "Reorganizes Estimate" from the backward stance of the tomb. From the end, we see "what We saw not" and do not see "What We saw before." Then, time and eternity, the finite and infinite, together form a "Compound Vision." Time, seen retrospectively, emerges as a continuum forward toward the God who directs it. With such a retrogressive progression the relative place of each moment emerges into cohesive shape.

The relative value of each moment emerges as well. "Admirations" become distinguished from "Contempts." Each event is not only organized and integrated but also weighed and judged. The tomb is more than the last point in a continuum from which to look back. It constitutes and encompasses all time at once. Not just end, but end as synecdochic wholeness provides the retrospective stance that makes forward motion possible and that determines its axiology. And only such final totality allows time's "Contempts" to be borne. The temporal differentiation that Dickinson found so unacceptable and that seemed a continual incremental loss would be justified only if it were a function of temporal wholeness. "Chaos" is described in one poem as a voyage in which there is not "even a Report of Land—/To justify—Despair" (#510). Without terminus, the journey seems senseless; and terminus must, as well, be validating. Final stance finally serves as the only redemption from traumas which Dickinson felt to be absolute, even as they were daily.

—Wolosky, Shira. "A Syntax of Contention." In *A Voice of War.* New Haven: Yale University Press, 1984.

JOAN BURBICK ON EMILY DICKINSON AND THE ECONOMICS OF DESIRE

[Joan Burbick is professor of English and American studies at Washington State University. She is the author of *Thoreau's Alternative History: Changing Perspectives on Nature, Culture and Language,* and *Healing the Republic: The Language of Health and Culture of Nationalism in Nineteenth-Century America.*]

Dickinson's most insidious voice involves the cost of desire as nothing less than death. Instead of displaying the scars of renunciation or remorse, Dickinson's speakers require death as the response to the mere thought of desire. Enthralling fantasies instantly kill (#1291) and thrust the speaker into a deadly landscape of economic measure: "Utmost is relative—/Have not or Have/Adjacent Sums/Enough—the first Abode/On the familiar Road/Galloped in Dreams—." Desire for Dickinson's speakers, as for the heroines of

Kate Chopin and Edith Wharton, ruins life and destroys the female body through suicide or fantasies of extinction.

Dickinson also writes poems, however, in which the death of the desiring self becomes the necessary prerequisite to prove love. "The Test of Love—is Death—" (#573) refers not only to the religious paradigm of Jesus's willingness to sacrifice his life for love, but also to the reality of "death" as the event which verifies desire. In another strangely tormented poem, the speaker urgently insists that her love can be proved in the face of impending doom. While the speaker watches the waters rise, threatening her extinction, the negation of her life is proof of love: "Oh Lover—Life could not convince—/ Might Death—enable Thee—" (#537).

Again, the cost of realizing desire is precisely self-annihilation. Desire is a fatal emotion for many Dickinson speakers; in a sense, it is much more dangerous than the Oedipal struggle. Whereas the son is threatened with castration, the daughter is threatened with the destruction of the entire body. The woman, of course, cannot be restrained through the cutting of a part. Her body in its entirety must be suppressed if she is to be made sexually ineffective. In working through the maze of wanting and the obstacles to desire, the woman must chart a system of punishment that does not seek to diminish power but to annihilate the body. The wounds on the body that "commemorate" its death are indeed the greatest threat to the attainment of desire. To want is to face intimately the "subtle suitor," Death. Put another way, what Dickinson seems to describe with unhalting repetition is the fact that restraint in its logical extreme demands as its price the total cancellation of the body.

Another variant to this economy that demands death for desire is the expression of desire in relation to the dead body. In some poems, the speaker imagines a space and time in which restraint from desire evaporates and the articulation of desire is allowed, if what one wants is dead. In a relatively early poem, Dickinson establishes how to "value" the lover without the presence of inhibiting restraint:

> As by the dead we love to sit,
> Become so wondrous dear—
> As for the lost we grapple
> Tho' all the rest are here—

In broken mathematics
We estimate our prize
Vast—in its fading ratio
To our penurious eyes! (#88)

In the language of exchange and measure, the other increases in price as it recedes into death. In a simple economy of desire, death ironically enhances the value of the desired: the corpse is most precious. In death all desire can be thought and spoken, freeing the speaker's voice to "value" the lover; but, of course, once spoken it cannot be acted upon in any other way than the drama of necrophilia. Basically, it frees only the voice: speakers are allowed to speak the words of desire to the dead precisely because they are dead and outside human action. In this way Dickinson describes how death ironically sanctions desire but forbids its consummation.

Some of Dickinson's speakers, however, often seek to outwit the threat of death. They envision a union of loved ones in the grave. Possession of the dead by the dead is a grim solution to an overwhelming social demand for the denial of pleasure:

If I may have it, when it's dead,
I'll be contented—so—
If just as soon as Breath is out
It shall belong to me—

Until they lock it in the Grave,
'Tis Bliss I cannot weigh—
For 'tho they lock Thee in the Grave,
Myself—can own the key— (#577)

—Burbick, Joan. "Emily Dickinson and the Economics of Desire." In *On Dickinson*. Durham, NC: Duke University Press, 1990.

CYNTHIA GRIFFIN WOLFF ON IMPERTINENT CONSTRUC-
TION OF BODY AND SELF: DICKINSON'S USE OF THE
ROMANTIC GROTESQUE

[Cynthia Griffin Wolff is the author of *Emily Dickinson* (1986).]

Once upon a time, most Dickinson scholars took it for granted that the poetry was a direct, unmediated reflection of "Emily Dickinson's state of mind" (whatever they thought it to be) and made no distinction between the speaking "I" of the verse and the woman herself. Today, we are more sophisticated and can reject such modes of misreading: "For all its value in the teacher's preparation," a modern scholar has recently written, "the historical, biographical, and ideological setting of Dickinson's work is something for our student to work toward, not work from."

One must applaud this advance; nonetheless, I wonder whether we have not gone too far in the opposite direction—whether in our sophistication we are missing something when we do not respond to the *apparently* "biographical" element in the poetry. Many naive admirers of Dickinson's work still have a curious preoccupation with her personal effects and her corporeal remains (the one white dress that is believed to have been hers, even the one lock of her dark red hair that is lodged in the archives at Amherst College and sometimes reverentially displayed during her birthday week in December); and the proprietors of Emily Dickinson's material estate preserve and display intimate, personal items with the same attention that they give to manuscripts, almost as if there were some obscure, but intrinsic connection. This attitude is different from the response evoked by other major authors, and if Dickinson's *scholars* generally distinguish between the speaker in a given poem and "Emily Dickinson herself," the ordinary citizens who still flood into the Dickinson home continue to think they have heard the woman in the work. Perhaps they are in touch with something "real," a unique, "Dickinsonian" tonality.

More than thirty years ago, Archibald MacLeish commented upon this illusion:

> No one can read these poems . . . without perceiving that he is not so much reading as being spoken to. There is a curious energy in the words and a tone like no other most of us have ever heard. Indeed, it is the tone rather than the words that one remembers afterwards.

Which is why one comes to a poem of Emily's one has never read before as to an old friend.

MacLeish has conflated a series of separate constructs (the poem, the "speaker" of the poem, and the "author") with the flesh-and-blood *person* who wrote the verse. And while this is undoubtedly a mistake in poetic analysis, it *does* respond to the vividness—the perhaps unmatched intensity of Dickinson's work.

Dickinson had a lean, mean imagination, and her irreverent humor slips like a whippet throughout the work: she loved riddles and jokes, and seems to have enjoyed making the speaking "self" (and its illusion of corporeal reality) the most profound riddle (or joke) of all. Thus her verse is saturated with the first person singular: "Poem after poem— more than a hundred and fifty of them—begins with the word 'I,' the talker's word. Moreover, there are body parts scattered throughout: one need only consult the *Concordance* entries for "hand," "hair," "foot," "brain," and the like to document this phenomenon. (The most extravagant proliferation can be found with "eye" and "eyes"—those playful puns for self; there are almost two hundred entries for them, one of the longest lists in the book!) Dickinson assaults us with "identity" at the same time that she deliberately baffles us with it; and if we entirely ignore issues of "author," "speaker," and their relationship to the "person, Emily Dickinson" ("self" and all of the [im]pertinent constructions of self), we may be missing something important.

Fundamentally, the big question can be construed as an issue of grammar: what is the referent for "I"? Readers who have responded intuitively, to "the author" or "Emily Dickinson"—and who have presumed that these entities are the same—feel that they have "heard" the "author" by virtue of having read the work; moreover, even when this "I" has an extravagant, carnivalesque component, it still tugs at many sleeves and seems to demand human recognition (this is one of her tricks). The compelling illusion of intimacy (along with the singular appearance of the verse upon the page—the unique "*skeleton*" of the poems) may be the most "Dickinsonian" element of the work. How, then, can we understand the force and intimacy of "I" in Dickinson's work without falling into simplistic confusions?

—Wolff, Cynthia Griffin. "[Im]pertinent Constructions of Body and Self: Dickinson's Use of the Romantic Grotesque." In *The Emily Dickinson Journal* 2 (1993).

Thematic Analysis of
"Tell all the Truth but tell it slant" (#1129)

The nature of Dickinson's truth is necessarily obscure. She wrote to a cousin, "It is true that the unknown is the largest need of the intellect, though for it, no one thinks to thank God" (Sewall, *Dickinson*, p. 161). The indirection she bore in her life and in her poetry allowed her to approach truth without becoming blinded by its brightness.

To a friend she wrote, "So I conclude that space & time are things of the body and have little or nothing to do with our selves. My Country is Truth" (Sewall, *Dickinson*, p. 10). She grants truth the status of a proper noun and removes it from the here and now. She has built a world, or rather a country, and called it Truth.

Although her poems follow some of the meters of English hymns, particularly those of Isaac Watts, Dickinson disregarded traditional poetic formulations. Custom required exact patterns and rhymes; she worked in slant rhymes and fitful punctuation. "When I try to organize—my little Force explodes," she wrote to Higginson when he complained that her poetry lacked form (Sewall, *Dickinson*, p. 240). Laboring endlessly over the same material, sometimes creating new meanings, sometimes adding, sometimes subtracting, Dickinson may have been disjunctive and ungrammatical, but she was never accidental.

Dickinson never set up solid symbolic structures, such as, for example, the equation of fire to love. This is not to say that she used no discernible frame of reference, but her lack of symbolic uniformity from poem to poem creates another barrier to her meaning.

Dickinson arrived on the American literary scene just as Ralph Waldo Emerson, Henry David Thoreau, Herman Melville, and Nathaniel Hawthorne were publishing their most influential works. In 1857, when Emerson lectured in Amherst and stayed with Dickinson's brother in his house next door, she felt "as if he had come from where dreams are born" (Bloom, *Dickinson*, p. 3). She appropriated Emerson's ideas about transcendent man as the ultimate reality, making a Truth all her own. Irreverent to the Puritan conception of deity, she called God "Burglar! Banker—Father!" (#49). This impertinence belies her concept of the Godhead and her intimate relationship with heaven, hell, and immortality.

Before Dickinson was twenty, she had rejected the notions of Christian sin and redemption. She retreated from the small evangelical community in Amherst with her own brand of religiosity and became a congregation of one. Understanding that the Bible's quest is for redemption rather than for truth or the sublime, Dickinson looked to poetry to shape that "superb surprise" that threatens to blind us. She needed to distinguish her concerns from strictly biblical ones, which "dealt with the Centre, not with Circumference—" (Bloom, *Dickinson*, p. 4). What was the limit that defined humanity? Not Emerson's; she would not accept his compensatory philosophy or his strident optimism.

Her Truth exists outside time. It is only partly available only part of the time. The complete revelation will come after life has gone.

> The Moments of Dominion
> That happen on the Soul
> And leave it with a Discontent
> Too exquisite—to tell— (#627)

The religious moment leaves discontentment in its wake, an exquisite discontentment that she struggles openly to articulate. These divine taunts were probably very real to Dickinson; her frustration wells up in such poems as #621:

> I asked no other thing—
> No other—was denied—
> I offered Being—for it—
> The Mighty Merchant sneered—
>
> Brazil? He twirled a Button—
> Without a glance my way—
> "But—Madam—is there nothing else—
> That We can show—Today?"

Nothing is denied her except the truth she longs for, and so she offers herself or her poetry, which she equates with Brazil, a symbol of exotic strangeness. The Mighty Merchant does not find her offering sufficient, however. This is certainly not Emerson's benevolent Transcendentalism. Emerson denied any such thing as a human circumference, insisting that we only limit ourselves; this limit was Dickinson's terrain precisely.

I saw no Way—The Heavens were stitched—
I felt the Columns close—
The Earth reversed her Hemispheres—
I touched the Universe—

And back it slid—and I alone—
A Speck upon a Ball—
Went out upon Circumference—
Beyond the Dip of Bell— (#378)

Toward the end of her life, Dickinson wrote in a letter, "To have lived is a Bliss so powerful—we must die—to adjust it." She delighted in reversing the doctrine of heavenly reward. As with her vision of truth, she ascribed an intensity to her vision of life that is so strong it cannot be encountered without consequences. Dickinson kept her circle of friends and family at a disturbing distance, allowing that slant angle to permeate her existence. She suffered from exaggerated perception and found any confrontational experience, whether it involved people or poems, overwhelming. She described the experience of poetry thus: "I feel physically as if the top of my head were taken off." She wrote to her friends longing to see them and then ran upstairs when they came to visit. (This may have been pathological, but it is important not to oversimplify her malady. To reduce her to a mere madwoman obliterates our attempt to reach her.) It was because of her profound sympathy and love for her friends that their physical presence (their "Truth") overwhelmed her.

Dickinson uncovers her sense of mission, of being a poet. What could be a larger task than to "tell all the Truth"? This poem is as much about the task of poetry as it is about her life and her truth. Dickinson wrote many poems that were self-consciously about the writing of poetry, a vocation she placed above God.

I reckon—when I count at all—
First—Poets—Then the Sun—
Then Summer—Then the Heaven of God—
And then—the List is done—

In fact, she gives God a rather low rank in her universe. She then revises her position in the next stanza when she considers that all of these components are really one and the same:

But, looking back—the First so seems
To Comprehend the Whole—

The Others look a needless Show—
So I write—Poets—All— (#569)

Not only is the poet the means to gaining truth—the poet is truth. Dickinson's placement of poetry as supreme is not an arrogant pronouncement of herself. In the context of her paradoxical mindset, it is quite the opposite, poised as she always was, "between skepticism and faith, desire and renunciation, optimism and despair." ❀

Critical Views on
"Tell all the Truth but tell it slant" (#1129)

HENRY W. WELLS ON ROMANTIC SENSIBILITY

[Henry W. Wells is the author of *Poet and Psychiatrist: Merrill Moore* and *Poetic Imagery, Illustrated from Elizabethan Literature.*]

The contrasted seeds of mysticism and Stoicism took root in Emily's mind not only because of her own personality, but through a congenial ground prepared for them by romantic sensibility. From a remote past ultimately came the two of her most precious heritages. But from her own cultural age she prudently drew what it had best to give. In view of her total accomplishments she is neither a mystic nor a stoic poet, though she undeniably is both mystical and stoical. Neither can her total achievement be labelled or confined by such descriptive epithets as classical, romantic, or modern. In some degree answering to each specification, her total stature can best be described in the phrase shrewdly noted by her biographer: "This was a poet." Nevertheless for a rounded appreciation of her art, recognition of its definitely romantic quality is essential, since no major aspect of her work can be properly grasped while others are disregarded. Her mind was integrated at least to the extent that such qualities as her peculiar mysticism and Stoicism are themselves properly explained only in the light of her romantic environment and soul.

Just as it is true that Emily remains far from wholly romantic, so it is clear that the whole of Romanticism in the historical sense is not to be traced in her own work. Singularly free from many of the qualities of her contemporaries or immediate predecessors, she has little specifically in common with the romantic poets, either of her own time of Tennyson, Browning, Swinburne, and Arnold, or the earlier period of Wordsworth, Coleridge, Keats, and Shelley. That she revolted from a Calvinistic training which she could never wholly forget, by no means makes her a follower of Byron, whose thought thus far, at least, followed hers. That she devoured Scott's tales, in no way allied her creative mind to the acknowledged master of the early nineteenth-century novel. She well knew that she followed her own star. Yet the popularity of her poems when first published, far surpassing the expectations of her editors and publishers, proves her to have been in some respects indigenous to her age. The woman who confessed that, whether with or against her will, she perforce saw "New Englandly," must have known that she also saw to some extent in the light of her age, coincident with the height of the Romantic Movement. Her conscious aims to remain the fresh imagination of childhood, to celebrate the self, to praise nature, and to indulge freely in fancy, stood among the most conspicuous ideals in the literature of her century. Although in the last analysis both her spirit and her style break violently with leading cultural patterns of the century, she was still its child, however naughty and rebellious. In no respect did she comply more closely than in cultivating the richest and most conspicuous vein in romantic thought as a whole, namely the new sensibility.

—Wells, Henry W. "Romantic Sensibility." In *Emily Dickinson: A Collection of Critical Essays,* Richard Sewall, ed. Englewood Cliffs, NJ: Prentice-Hall, Inc., 1963.

R. P. BLACKMUR ON EMILY DICKINSON'S NOTATION

[R. P. Blackmur, Professor of English at Princeton University, is the author of *Emily Dickinson's Poetry: Stairway of Surprise* and *Melville in the South Seas* and the editor of the centennial edition of *Sidney Lanier.*]

Some twenty years ago it was necessary to begin an essay on Emily Dickinson with a complaint that the manuscripts and the various copies of manuscripts of this poet had never been adequately edited, and could never be properly read until they were. It seems to me now—and the reviews I have seen agree—that Mr. Johnson has done everything an editor can do, and that there remains—and on this Mr. Johnson himself insists in his preface—the second task of providing a more readable, and less expensive, edition for the ordinary purposes of poetry. This I hope Mr. Johnson will undertake because, whoever undertakes it, it will be the completion of Mr. Johnson's own work; and because it will itself be a criticism of Emily Dickinson's work at almost every possible level. The principal problem, it seems to me, will be to find within the general conventions of printing a style of presentation which will furnish a version conformable to the original notation which the poet employed. The Dickinson practice was to punctuate by dashes, as if the reader would know what the dashes meant—both grammatically and dramatically—by giving the verses voice. Within her practice, and to her own ear, she was no doubt consistent. To find out what that consistence was, and to articulate it for other readers and other voices, requires more of a system than ever bothered her. Even a casual examination of any twenty pages in this new edition makes this aspect of the problem plain. Here is an example to do for the rest.

> Some—work for Immortality—
> The chiefer part, for Time—
> He—Compensates—immediately—
> The former—Checks—on Fame—

The Dickinson practice cannot be systematized; there is not enough *there*; but with enough intimacy with the poems we can see what sort of system might have emerged. The problem is not very different, so I understand, in reading the official prose of Japan in 1875; but in English poetry it seldom presents itself with such multiplicity of irritation—so much freedom in rearrangement—with such spontaneity left to the reader.

Multiplicity, freedom, spontaneity: these are terms for much deeper aspects of the Dickinson notation than that which gathers itself in mere punctuation, syntax and grammar; or in meter, rhythm, and diction. Perhaps the deepest problem in poetics raises one of its prettiest examples in her notation. How much does a poet look to words to supply what is put down, and how much to notate what was within the self prior to the words? If words are necessarily the medium of poetry, how much do they also participate in its substance? If thought looks for words as a chief medium for turning it into action, how much, if anything, of the action is in the movement of the words themselves? Is there not in the end a nearly equal contest between the thought prior to the words and the thought already reminiscent in the words and their arrangements? If so, victory for the poet will be in the equilibrium between the two; what is in W. B. Cannon's physiology the maintenance of a precarious stable state, or homeostasis, called the wisdom of the body. This equilibrium, this wisdom, is in poetry recorded, though it is not maintained; is communicated, though it does not exist—in the words taken as notation. In this respect the words resemble the notes in music.

The words resemble the notes on the musical score. This is not said as a triviality but as a fact about poetry and music that no theory can ultimately ignore. It is said that Beethoven sometimes wrote out his initial score in words, and surely there are some poems where the words seem like the notes in a final score—as perhaps "The Phoenix and the Turtle." There is only a difference in the degree of notation. The point is that the notation is always inadequate, by itself, in predicting performance or reading. As the poet was saying much more, so the reader is left with more or less to do for himself as the notation wills him or fails him. This is why the poem which has seemed flat will spring into life when one has got intimate with that will. My friends the composers tell me that the notation in music is perhaps eighty-five per cent adequate, which seems to me high and can only be true of modern music (the music the composers themselves wrote). In poetry I am convinced the notation is at best only about fifteen per cent adequate for a full reading; the gaps jumped are *that* much greater; and indeed a single reading can never again be more than approximately repeated, and as the approximations go on, the life of the poem thickens in the reader's mind and throat. The uniqueness of each reading reaches towards the uniqueness of the poem. Thus the poet's own reading, like his own notation, is often inadequate to the poem; his voice no more than his words is not up to a final job, but yet always should be heard. We cannot do without as much of the feasible fifteen per cent as we can get from the poet or can, after sufficient intimacy, otherwise arrange for. In Emily Dickinson's case the notation in the words seldom reaches the feasible maximum even with intimacy; and it is here, I think, that the final problem of critical editorship lies, since we must not permit ourselves to lose the record of our intimacy. The editor must learn to notate the voice which in intimacy he has learned to hear; which is not at all the same thing as notating merely what he has learned to understand. Consider why Toscanini is a great conductor, and then consider how Emily Dickinson's poems, all short, have none of the self-modulating advantages of length or any of the certainties of complex overt structure. One exaggerates, but it sometimes seems as if in her work a cat came at us speaking

English, our own language, but without the pressure of all the other structures we are accustomed to attend; it comes at us all voice so far as it is in control, fragmented elsewhere, willful and arbitrary, because it has not the acknowledged means to be otherwise.

—Blackmur, R. P. "Emily Dickinson's Notation." In *The Kenyon Review* 18 (1956).

CHARLES R. ANDERSON ON WORDS

[Charles R. Anderson retired in 1969 as Caroline Donovan Professor of English at Johns Hopkins University. Besides his work on Dickinson, he is known for his writings on Melville, Thoreau, and Henry James.]

Another technique, thought of as peculiarly Dickinsonian, is of course the way of all poetry—by indirection. But the oblique approach, the sudden and unexpected turn, becomes such a pervasive habit as to constitute her unique mode of expression. "Tell all the Truth but tell it slant," she says, for it must be perceived and revealed gradually or it will dazzle into blindness. A passage in Emerson's "Uriel" may have suggested the metaphor by which she justifies the circuitous approach:

> Too bright for our inform Delight
> The Truth's superb surprise.

Slant and surprise, the distinctive marks of her best poetry, are the result of her brilliant verbal strategy. A kinship, rather than an influence, is revealed by the analogies that can be drawn from Emerson's *Poems,* one of her most cherished possessions being the copy given her in 1850 by the friend who first awakened her mind and creative powers. There she could have read, in "Merlin" the archetypal poet, the best possible epigraph for her own poetic achievement:

> He shall aye climb
> For his rhyme ...
> But mount to paradise
> By the stairway of surprise.

Concerned with expression from her earliest years, she is clearly referring to her need for freedom in finding her own voice when she complains in one of her poems: "They shut me up in Prose." "They" were all the forces that militated against her being a poet. Living in a family of practical people and in an isolated community, she had little encouragement to leave the common-sense ways of prose. What she said of her father in a letter of 1851 could be applied to her environment as a whole, that he was too intent on "real life" to have any interest in poetry. Similarly, at about the same time, she wrote to one of her few companions in wit and literature: "[We] please ourselves with the fancy that we are the only poets, and everyone else is *prose*." Prose to her was limited, as the similes in the poem put it, like being shut up in a closet when a girl so she would be "still," or like putting a bird in prison. If they had only peeped and seen her "brain go round," she says, they would have known she had the madness of a poet who would not stay shut up in convention. The true singer breaks out of any prison, as the bird by an effort of will abolishes his captivity and sings. So she too, even in the letters which were virtually her only medium of expression until about the age of twenty-eight, broke out of the narrow limits of prose into poetic freedoms that make it hard to draw a line between her use of the two modes. "They shut me up in Prose" may also refer to the conventional kind of verse her mentors urged upon her when she finally did venture into poetry. For this poem was written at the very end of 1862, after that first remarkable exchange with Higginson, the only letters in which they seriously discussed artistic problems. She soon put him down as another of those who would shut her up in prose, whom she must escape if she wanted to mount the stairway of surprise.

—Anderson, Charles R. *"Words."* In *Emily Dickinson's Poetry: The Stairway of Surprise.* New York: Holt, Rinehart and Winston, 1960.

RICHARD WILBUR ON "SUMPTUOUS DESTITUTION"

[Richard Wilbur's books of poetry include *The Beautiful Changes, Things of This World,* and *New and Collected Poems.* He collaborated with Lillian Hellman on the comic opera *Candide* and has translated Voltaire, Racine, and Molière. *Responses* is a collection of his critical essays.]

Emily Dickinson elected the economy of desire, and called her privation good, rendering it positive by renunciation. And so she came to live in a huge world of delectable distances. Far-off words like "Brazil" or "Circassian" appear continually in her poems as symbols of things distanced by loss or renunciation, yet infinitely prized and yearned-for. So identified in her mind are distance and delight that, when ravished by the sight of a hummingbird in her garden, she calls it "the mail from Tunis." And not only are the objects of her desire distant; they are also very often moving away, their sweetness increasing in proportion to their remoteness. "To disappear enhances," one of the poems begins, and another closes with these lines:

> The Mountain—at a given distance—
> In Amber—lies—
> Approached—the Amber flits—a little—
> And That's—the Skies— (#572)

To the eye of desire, all things are seen in a profound perspective, either moving or gesturing toward the vanishing-point. Or to use a figure which may be closer to Miss Dickinson's thought, to the eye of desire the world is a centrifuge, in which all things are straining or flying toward the occult circumference. In some such way, Emily Dickinson conceived her world, and it was in a spatial metaphor that she gave her personal definition of Heaven. "Heaven," she said, "is what I cannot reach."

At times it seems that there is nothing in her world but her own soul, with its attendant abstractions, and, at a vast remove, the inscrutable Heaven. On most of what might intervene she has closed the valves of her attention, and what mortal objects she does acknowledge are riddled by desire to the point of transparency. Here is a sentence from her correspondence: "Enough is of so vast sweetness, I suppose it never occurs, only pathetic counterfeits." The writer of that sentence could not invest her longings in any finite object. Again she wrote, "Emblem is immeasurable—that is why it is better than fulfillment, which can be drained." For such a sensibility, it was natural and necessary that things be touched with infinity. Therefore her nature poetry, when most serious, does not play descriptively with birds or flowers but presents us repeatedly with dawn, noon, and sunset, those grand ceremonial moments of the day which argue the splendor of Paradise. or it shows us the ordinary landscape transformed by the electric brilliance of a storm; or it shows us the fields succumbing to the annual mystery of death. In her love-poems, Emily Dickinson was at first covetous of the beloved himself; indeed, she could be idolatrous, going so far as to say that his face, should she see it again in Heaven, would eclipse the face of Jesus. But in what I take to be her later work the beloved's lineaments, which were never very distinct, vanish entirely; he becomes pure emblem, a symbol of remote spiritual joy, and is all but absorbed into the idea of Heaven.

—Wilbur, Richard. "Sumptuous Destitution." In *Emily Dickinson: Three Views*, with Louise Bogan and Archibald MacLeish. Amherst, MA: Amherst College Press, 1960.

LOUISE BOGAN ON A MYSTICAL POET

[Louise Bogan, poet and critic, is the author of *Achievement in American Poetry* and *Selected Criticism*.]

One of the dominant facts concerning Emily Dickinson is her spirit of religious unorthodoxy. Her deeply religious feeling ran outside the bounds of dogma; this individualism was, in fact, an inheritance from her Calvinist forbears, but it was out of place when contrasted to the Evangelicanism to which, in her time, so many Protestants had succumbed. She early set herself against the guilt and gloom inherent in this revivalism. She avoided the constrictions which a narrow insistence on religious rule and law would put upon her. She had read Emerson with delight, but, as Yvor Winters has remarked, it is a mistake to think of her as a Transcendentalist in dimity. Here again she worked through to a standpoint and an interpretation of her own; her attitude toward pain and suffering, toward the shocking facts of existence, was far more realistic than Emerson's. As we examine her chief spiritual preoccupations, we see how closely she relates to the English Romantic poets who, a generation or so before her, fought a difficult and unpopular battle against the eighteenth century's cold logic and mechanical point of view. The names of Blake and Coleridge come to mind; we know that to both these poets the cold theory of Locke represented "a deadly heresy on the nature of existence." It is difficult to look back to this period of early Romantic breakthrough, since so much of that early boldness and originality was later dissipated in excesses of various kinds. But it is important to remember that Blake attached the greatest importance to the human imagination as an aspect of some mystery beyond the human, and to listen to his ringing words: "The world of Imagination is the world of Eternity. . . . The world of Imagination is Infinite and Eternal, whereas the world of generation is Finite and Temporal"—and to remember, as well, that "Blake, Wordsworth, Coleridge, Shelley and Keats shared the belief that the imagination was nothing less than God as he operates in the human soul." C. M. Bogan, writing of the Romantic ethos in general, brings out a fact which has been generally overlooked: that, although Romantic poetry became a European phenomenon, English Romantic poetry "almost alone . . . connected visionary insight with a superior order of being." "There is hardly a trace of this [insight]," Bowra goes on to say, "in Hugo, or Heine or Lermontov. They have their full share of longing, but almost nothing of Romantic vision." Hölderlin, in Germany tried to share a lost vision of Greece, but on the whole it was the English who accomplished a transformation in thought and emotion "for which there is no parallel in their age." It is surely in the company of these English poets that Emily Dickinson belongs. At its most intense, her vision not only matched, but transcended theirs; she crossed the same boundaries with a like intransigence; and the same vigorous flowers sprang from different seeds, in the spirit of a woman born in 1830, in New England, in America.

—Bogan, Louise. "A Mystical Poet." In *Emily Dickinson: Three Views,* with Richard Wilbur and Archibald MacLeish. Amherst, MA: Amherst College Press, 1960

ANTHONY HECHT ON THE RIDDLES OF EMILY DICKINSON

[Anthony Hecht has written *The Hard Hours, The Venetian Vespers, The Transparent Man,* and other volumes of poetry, for which he has received the Pulitzer Prize, the Bollingen Prize, and the Prix de Rome. He is also the author of two critical studies, *Obbligati* and *The Hidden Law: The Poetry of W. H. Auden.*]

> Tell all the Truth but tell it slant—
> Success in Circuit lies
> Too bright for our infirm Delight
> The Truth's superb surprise
> As Lightning to the Children eased
> With explanation kind
> The Truth must dazzle gradually
> Or every man be blind—

Again, this poem has been read as an instance of Emily Dickinson's deliberate tact and poetic strategy "in a generation which did not permit her, without the ambiguity of the riddle, to 'tell the truth' . . . she early learned that 'success in circuit lies.'" I cannot disprove that notion, nor do I feel obliged to; but the poem seems to me to have a good deal of religious significance that such a statement inclines altogether to flout.

> And it came to pass on the third day in the morning, that there were thunders and lightning and thick clouds upon the mount. . . . And the Lord said unto Moses, Go down, charge the people, lest they break through unto the Lord to gaze, and many of them perish.
>
> (Exodus 19:16–21)

The blinding effect of direct access to the Godhead, which is to say the Truth (except in the case of selected few, and Moses one of them), has been a commonplace of religious poetry from long before Emily Dickinson to our own century. And there is what might be called a New Testament version of the same idea. Jesus has just told his followers the parable of the sower and the seed:

And he said unto them, He that hath ears to hear, let him hear. And when he was alone, they that were about him with the twelve asked of him the parable.

And he said unto them, Unto you is given to know the mystery of the kingdom of God: but unto them that are without, all these things are done in parables.

(Mark 4:9–11)

Christ himself has been seen as that human manifestation of the Godhead which allows all men to look upon that Truth which would otherwise be blinding. Milton clearly has such a meditating notion in mind in the "Nativity Ode."

> That glorious form, that light insufferable,
> And that far-beaming blaze of majesty,
> Wherewith he wont at Heaven's high council-table
> To sit the midst of Trinal Unity,
> He laid aside; and here with us to be,
> Forsook the courts of everlasting day,
> And chose with us a darksome house of mortal clay.

The same idea is, as I understand it, somewhat blasphemously paralleled by John Donne in "The Extasie," in which, like Christ undergoing human incarnation, the Truth and the Word becoming flesh, so must the pure lovers' "souls descend/T'affections and to faculties," and he continues, "To our bodies turne we then, that so/ Weak men on love revealed may look."

I am not asserting an influence of either Milton or Donne on Emily Dickinson. I am, however, convinced that the success that lies in circuit, that dictates that all the truth must be told, but told slant, has behind it the authority of both the Old and New Testament: that parables, riddles, the Incarnation itself are but aspects of a Truth we could not comprehend without their mediation.

—Hecht, Anthony. "The Riddle of Emily Dickinson." In *Obbligati*. New York: Atheneum, 1986.

[Cristanne Miller is professor of English at Pomona College, author of *Emily Dickinson: A Poet's Grammar*, and coauthor (with Suzanne Juhasz and Martha Nell Smith) of *Comic Power in Emily Dickinson.*]

Slanted truth and disjunctive language, like the pretense that she is conveyor of nature's "News," protect the writer from having to bear full responsibility for her messages. Complex and elliptical language is not immediately understood. Readers of Dickinson's poems and letters may doubt all they read in her cryptic ambiguity, and thus not blame the poet for saying what they do not want to hear from her. She is protected from sounding as radical or rebellious as she often is because understanding those aspects of her writing requires some complicity from her reader; since readers must work at understanding her texts, they must therefore to some extent be capable of recognizing a possibility of meaning before they can find it. The differences between late nineteenth century and modern readings of several poems show how extremely reader receptivity may affect the interpretation of a poem. Only after a reader becomes sensitive to, for example, gendered possibilities of meaning are those elements of Dickinson's poems recognized. The opacity and multiplicity of the language likewise prevent—or allow—readers who do not recognize gender as an element of perception to overlook entirely that aspect of her poems while feeling confident about their reading. The poems' linguistic and metaphorical complexity allows Dickinson's readers to see her truths only as they are capable of admitting them.

Because, somewhat paradoxically, distorted language or communication at a distance increases Dickinson's willingness to speak, writing provides an avenue for more intimate and passionate expression than she feels comfortable with face to face. This is a truth all letter writers know. Even more than talking in the dark, writing letters allows private feelings to be articulated in a language half art, half hyperbole, with the assurance that these feelings will be heard and the safety of not being watched while they are spoken. In person, the poet could scarcely have said: "Thank you for having been"; or "I should be wild with joy to see my little lovers. The writing them is not so sweet as their two faces that seem so small way off, and yet have been two weeks from me—two wishful, wandering weeks"; or in the much-corrected draft of a letter to Otis Lord:

> Dont you know you are happiest while I withhold and not confer—
> dont you know that "No" is the wildest word we consign to Language?
> . . . It is Anguish I long conceal from you to let you leave me, hungry, but you ask the divine Crust and that would doom the Bread.
> That unfrequented Flower

In writing from a distance, Dickinson may give all in language that she withholds in fact. This returns us full circle to the poet's own excuse for including poems in prose: "Because I could not say it—I fixed it in the verse—for you to read." From the greater distance of poetic "letters" or language more formally patterned and constrained than her prose, she may play out thoughts and feelings that have no easily expressed place in her life.

> —Miller, Cristanne. "Letters to the World." In *Emily Dickinson: A Poet's Grammar.* Cambridge, MA: Harvard University Press, 1989.

JEROME MCGANN ON EMILY DICKINSON'S VISIBLE LANGUAGE

[Jerome McGann is the John Stewart Bryan Professor of English at the University of Virginia. Among his works are *Black Riders, The Visible Language of Modernism,* and *The New Oxford Book of Romantic Period Verse.*]

In the letter to Higginson, on the other hand, the poem is copied according to what Higginson himself called "the habit of freedom and the unconventional utterance of daring thoughts." In truth, however, Dickinson's text in the letter is by no means "unconventional." Rather, it is a poetical text that exploits the writing resources—the conventions—of epistolary intercourse. So when Higginson speaks of her writing as "Wayward and unconventional in the last degree; defiant of form, measure, rhyme, and even grammar," his judgment reflects his expectations about the appropriate "conventions" that should govern a poet's work.

Following Emerson, Higginson classified Dickinson's work as "The Poetry of the Portfolio": private writing "not meant for publication." This judgment seems to me exact if we understand the specific historicality of Higginson's remark; if we understand that in the late nineteenth-century "publication" only came when a poet followed certain textual conventions. These conventions—they are strictly bibliographical rather than more broadly formal—were so dominant that most poets and readers could not imagine poetry without them. (Tennyson and D. G. Rossetti, for example, both said that they could not really begin to see their own poetry until it was put into print!) Higginson's response to Dickinson's writing as "spasmodic" and "uncontrolled" reflects these habits of thought.

But the writing is not spasmodic or uncontrolled or defiant of form. It has instead chosen to draw its elementary rules of form by an analogy to the writing conventions of personal correspondence rather than to the conventions of the printed text.

Up to now Dickinson's editors, as well as the vast majority of her readers, have not understood this crucial formality of her work. The poem Dickinson sent to Higginson in her letter of 7 June 1862 is run into the text of the "prose." In Johnson, this scene of writing is bibliographically translated. For the poem, Johnson's edition of the *Letters* puts into print an equivalent of the text Dickinson wrote in fascicle 1. In the letter she rewrites her earlier text—the fascicle text Higginson hadn't seen—by following the options released through a scriptural and epistolary environment rather than a publishing and biographical one. No doubt Higginson would have approved the fascicle 1 text: after Dickinson's death, when he first saw the fascicles, he was surprised (he said) to find that so many of the poems "have *form* beyond most of those I have seen before." He says this because what he had "seen before"—the poems she sent to him in her letters—were all organized scripturally rather than bibliographically.

The poem in this letter is particularly important because the letter famously addresses the issue of publication. "I smile when you suggest that I delay 'to publish'—that being foreign to my thought, as Firmament to Fin." Dickinson is not writing to ask Higginson for professional help or for schooling in formal proprieties. She is aware that she has undertaken an unusual approach to poetical writing. The question she wants to ask him is different: given the choice she has made, is her work "clear?"

The answer she received was "yes," as we know from the continuation of their correspondence. Higginson understood, and his understanding is measured as much by his admiration for the force of her writing as it is by his dismay at her incorrigible incorrectnesses. So far as Dickinson was concerned, that doubled understanding—Higginson's blindness and insight alike—proved equally important to her life as a writer.

—McGann, Jerome. "Emily Dickinson's Visible Language." In *The Emily Dickinson Journal* 2 (1993).

Works by
Emily Dickinson

Emily Dickinson is known to have written 1,775 poems, none of which have titles. Thomas H. Johnson compiled the standard edition of the poems and numbered them according to their chronology.

Works about
Emily Dickinson

Anderson, Charles R. *Emily Dickinson's Poetry: Stairway of Surprise.* New York: Holt, Rinehart & Winston, 1960.

Barker, Wendy. *Lunacy of Light: Emily Dickinson and the Experience of Metaphor.* Carbondale: Southern Illinois University Press, 1987.

Bennett, Paula. *Emily Dickinson: Woman Poet.* Iowa City: University of Iowa Press, 1991.

Blake, Caesar R., and Carlton F. Wells, eds. *The Recognition of Emily Dickinson.* Ann Arbor: University of Michigan Press, 1964.

Bloom, Harold, ed. *Emily Dickinson: Modern Critical Views.* New York: Chelsea House, 1985.

Buckingham, Willis J. *Emily Dickinson's Reception in the 1890s: A Documentary History.* Pittsburgh: University of Pittsburgh Press, 1989.

Cady, Edwin H., and Louis J. Budd, eds. *On Dickinson: The Best from American Literature.* Durham, NC: Duke University Press, 1990.

Cameron, Sharon. *Lyric Time: Dickinson and the Limits of Genre.* Baltimore: The Johns Hopkins University Press, 1979.

———. *Choosing Not Choosing: Dickinson's Fascicles.* Chicago: University of Chicago Press, 1992.

Capps, Jack L. *Emily Dickinson's Reading: 1836–1886.* Cambridge, MA: Harvard University Press, 1966.

Cody, John. *After Great Pain: The Inner Life of Emily Dickinson.* Cambridge, MA: Harvard University Press, 1971.

Diehl, Joanne Feit. *Dickinson and the Romantic Imagination.* Princeton: Princeton University Press, 1981.

Dobson, Joanne. *Dickinson and the Strategies of Reticence: The Woman Writer in Nineteenth Century America.* Bloomington: Indiana University Press, 1989.

Eberwein, Jane Donahue. *Dickinson: Strategies of Limitation.* Amherst, MA: The University of Massachusetts Press, 1985.

Farr, Judith. *The Passion of Emily Dickinson.* Cambridge, MA: Harvard University Press, 1992.

Ferlazzo, Paul J., ed. *Critical Essays on Emily Dickinson.* Boston: G. K. Hall and Co., 1984.

Ford, Thomas W. Heaven *Beguiles the Tired: Death in the Poetry of Emily Dickinson.* Tuscaloosa: University of Alabama Press, 1966.

Franklin, R. W. *The Editing of Emily Dickinson: A Reconsideration.* Madison: University of Wisconsin Press, 1967.

Gelpi, Albert. *Emily Dickinson: The Mind of the Poet.* Cambridge, MA: Harvard University Press, 1966.

———. *The Tenth Muse.* Cambridge, MA: Harvard University Press, 1975.

Gilbert, Sandra M., and Susan Gubar. *The Madwoman in the Attic: The Woman Writer and the Nineteenth Century Literary Imagination.* New Haven: Yale University Press, 1979.

Griffith, Clark. *The Long Shadow: Emily Dickinson's Tragic Poetry.* Princeton: Princeton University Press, 1964.

Howe, Susan. *My Emily Dickinson.* Berkeley, CA: North Atlantic Books, 1985.

Johnson, Thomas. *Emily Dickinson: An Interpretive Biography.* Cambridge, MA: Harvard University Press, 1964.

Juhasz, Suzanne. "The Undiscovered Continent": *Emily Dickinson and the Space of the Mind.* Bloomington: Indiana University Press, 1983.

Juhasz, Suzanne, Cristanne Miller, and Martha Nell Smith. *Comic Power in Emily Dickinson.* Austin: University of Texas Press, 1993.

Keller, Karl. *The Only Kangaroo among the Beauty: Emily Dickinson and America.* Baltimore: The Johns Hopkins University Press, 1979.

Lease, Benjamin. *Emily Dickinson's Readings of Men and Books.* New York: St. Martin's Press, 1990.

Lindberg-Seyersted, Brita. *The Voice of the Poet: Aspects of Style in the Poetry of Emily Dickinson.* Cambridge, MA: Harvard University Press, 1968.

MacLeish, Archibald, Louise Bogan, and Richard Wilbur. *Emily Dickinson: Three Views.* Amherst, MA: Amherst College Press, 1960.

McGann, Jerome. *Black Riders: The Visible Language of Modernism.* Princeton, N.J.: Princeton University Press, 1993.

Miller, Cristanne. *Emily Dickinson: A Poet's Grammar.* Cambridge, MA: Harvard University Press, 1987.

Pollack, Vivian R. Dickinson: *The Anxiety of Gender.* Ithaca, NY: Cornell University Press, 1984.

Porter, David T. *The Art of Emily Dickinson's Early Poetry*. Cambridge, MA: Harvard University Press, 1966.

———. *Dickinson: The Modern Idiom*. Cambridge, MA: Harvard University Press, 1981.

Rosenbaum, S. P. *A Concordance to the Poems of Emily Dickinson*. Ithaca, NY: Cornell University Press, 1966.

St. Armand, Barton Levi. *Emily Dickinson and Her Culture: The Soul's Society*. Cambridge, MA: Cambridge University Press, 1984.

Sewall, Richard B., ed. *Emily Dickinson: A Collection of Critical Essays*. Englewood Cliffs, NJ: Prentice-Hall, 1963.

Sherwood, William Robert. *Circumference and Circumstance: Stages in the Mind and Art of Emily Dickinson*. New York: Columbia University Press, 1968.

Shurr, William R., ed. *New Poems of Emily Dickinson*. Chapel Hill: University of North Carolina Press, 1993.

Small, Judy Jo. *Positive as Sound: Emily Dickinson's Rhyme*. Athens, GA: University of Georgia Press, 1990.

Smith, Martha Nell. *Rowing in Eden: Rereading Emily Dickinson*. Austin: University of Texas Press, 1992.

Stonum, Gary Lee. *The Dickinson Sublime*. Madison: University of Wisconsin Press, 1993.

Weisbuch, Robert. *Emily Dickinson's Poetry*. Chicago: University of Chicago Press, 1975.

Whicher, George. *This Was a Poet*. New York: Charles Scribner's Sons, 1938.

Wolosky, Shira. *Emily Dickinson: A Voice of War*. New Haven: Yale University Press, 1984.

Index of
Themes and Ideas